HIRING FOR SUCCESS

Build Your Dream Team

DAVID M ARNOLD
Crystal Coast HR

This is a Blank Page

Disclaimer

The content provided in the "Hiring for Success: Build Your Dream Team" training program is for educational and informational purposes only. This program is designed to offer guidance on best practices in hiring, team building, and employee management. However, it should not be construed as legal, financial, or professional advice.

The creators and instructors of this course do not guarantee specific hiring outcomes, employee performance, or business success. Laws and regulations related to employment, hiring practices, and workplace management may vary by jurisdiction. We strongly recommend consulting with legal or HR professionals to ensure compliance with local, state, and federal laws before implementing any hiring strategies or policies discussed in this program.

By participating in this course, you acknowledge that you are responsible for your own hiring decisions and any consequences that may arise from them. The creators, instructors, and affiliates of this program disclaim any liability for losses, damages, or risks incurred as a result of applying the information provided.

For personalized advice or consultation, please seek the assistance of a qualified professional.

Copyright © 2024 David M Arnold | Crystal Coast HR | All rights reserved.

The content, materials, and intellectual property contained in this program, "Hiring for Success: Build Your Dream Team," are protected by copyright law. Unauthorized reproduction, distribution, modification, or any other use of the content, in whole or in part, without the express written permission of Crystal coast HR is strictly prohibited.

Any unauthorized use may result in legal action. For permissions or licensing requests, please contact Crystal Coast HR at Mike@CrystalCoastHR.com.

Acknowledgment

Creating this book would not have been possible without the support, encouragement, and insights from many individuals who contributed to its development.

First and foremost, I want to express my deepest gratitude to the small business owners and entrepreneurs who inspired this project. Your resilience, creativity, and passion for building something meaningful have been a constant source of motivation. I hope this guide serves as a valuable resource in your journey to success.

A special thank you goes to my family and friends for their unwavering support throughout the writing process. Your patience, understanding, and encouragement have been invaluable.

I would also like to acknowledge the experts and professionals who generously shared their knowledge and experiences. Your insights and feedback have helped shape the content of this book, making it a practical and actionable guide for readers.

To my editor and publishing team, thank you for your dedication, expertise, and meticulous attention to detail. Your guidance has been instrumental in bringing this project to life.

Lastly, I am grateful to you, the reader, for choosing this book. I hope the strategies and advice within these pages empower you to build a strong, effective team that drives your business forward.

Thank you all for being a part of this journey. Your support and belief in the vision of this book have made it possible.

Dedication

To the dreamers, the doers, and the small business owners who refuse to give up, even when the odds are stacked against you.

This book is dedicated to those who have taken the leap of faith to build something from the ground up, driven by passion, resilience, and the unwavering belief in the power of a great team.

May this guide help you find the right people to share in your journey, support your vision, and bring your dreams to life.

Here's to the entrepreneurs who know that success is not just about what you achieve, but who you surround yourself with along the way.

Table of Contents

Disclaimer 2
Acknowledgment 4
Dedication 6
Preface 11
Chapter 1: The Foundations of Hiring for Small Businesses 14
    Understanding Your Hiring Needs 15
    Identifying Key Roles and Skills Essential for Your Business 15
    Differentiating Between Full-Time, Part-Time, Freelance, and Remote Workers 16
    How to Attract Candidates Who Align with Your Business Vision 19
    Creating a Culture Fit Checklist to Screen Applicants 21
    Real-World Examples and Case Studies 23
Chapter 2: Crafting a Compelling Job Description.............. 26
    Best Practices for Crafting Job Descriptions 27
    Using SEO to Make Your Job Postings More Discoverable 35
Chapter 3: Cost-Effective Recruitment Strategies.............. 40
    Leveraging Free and Low-Cost Job Boards 41
    Networking and Employee Referrals 44
    Utilizing Social Media for Recruitment 46
    Hiring Interns and Entry-Level Candidates 49
    Developing an Internship Program 50
Chapter 4: Interviewing and Assessing Candidates............ 53
    Structuring Effective Interviews 54

Best Practices for Interview Structure 56
Assessing Soft Skills and Cultural Fit 57
Creating a Culture Fit Checklist 59
Using Skills Assessments and Trial Projects 60
Virtual Interviews and Remote Hiring 63
Tips for Assessing Remote Candidates 64

Chapter 5: Onboarding for Success 67
Creating an Engaging Onboarding Program 68
Setting Clear Expectations and Goals 71
Providing Continuous Training and Development 73
Using Technology for Training 76
The Role of Mentorship in Employee Success 77

Chapter 6: Leveraging Freelancers and Remote Workers ... 80
Benefits of Hiring Freelancers 81
Finding and Vetting Freelancers 84
Managing Remote Teams Effectively 87
Contract Workers vs. Full-Time Employees 89

Chapter 7: Employee Retention on a Budget 93
Building a Positive Work Environment 94
Offering Non-Monetary Perks and Benefits 97
Recognition Programs that Don't Break the Bank 99
Recognizing and Rewarding Performance 99
Budget-Friendly Training and Development Programs .. 103
Encouraging Continuous Learning 104

Chapter 8: Legal and Compliance Considerations 106
Drafting Employment Contracts 109

Avoiding Discrimination in Hiring 110

Avoiding Discriminatory Practices 112

Classifying Workers Correctly 113

Penalties for Misclassification 114

Keeping Up with HR Documentation 115

Implementing Document Retention Policies 117

Navigating Audits and Legal Requests 118

Chapter 9: Scaling Your Team as Your Business Grows 120

Knowing When to Hire 121

Planning for Seasonal and Project-Based Hiring 125

Building a Talent Pipeline 128

Outsourcing vs. In-House Hiring 131

Chapter 10: Leveraging Technology in Recruitment 134

Using Applicant Tracking Systems (ATS) 135

Automating the Hiring Process 139

Virtual Team-Building Tools 142

Data-Driven Hiring Decisions 146

Conclusion: Building Your Dream Team on a Budget 150

Recap of Key Takeaways 151

Encouragement to Take Action 157

Bonus Resources 162

Templates and Checklists 163

Interview Question Templates 165

Onboarding Checklist 167

Recommended Tools and Software 169

Team Management Tools 170

Productivity and Communication Tools 171
Further Reading and Online Courses 172

Preface

Building Your Dream Team on a Budget

As a small business owner, the path to success is often paved with challenges. One of the most important—and sometimes daunting—tasks you face is building a talented, dedicated team that can propel your business forward. Whether you're just starting out or have been in business for years, the need to assemble a skilled and motivated team is crucial. However, many small businesses struggle with limited resources, especially when it comes to hiring the right people.

This book is written for business owners like you—those who recognize the importance of building a great team but need to do so on a budget. Throughout this guide, I aim to provide practical, actionable strategies that will help you attract, hire, and retain top talent without breaking the bank.

You don't need a large budget to build a team of dedicated professionals. In fact, with the right strategies, tools, and mindset, you can create an environment where talented individuals will not only want to work for you but will remain loyal, motivated, and engaged. From creating compelling job descriptions and offering non-monetary perks to implementing streamlined hiring processes and utilizing technology, this book is designed to be your roadmap to effective, affordable team-building.

Each chapter is filled with real-world examples, step-by-step guides, and templates that will help you take immediate action. You'll learn how to plan for seasonal hiring, streamline your recruitment processes, leverage technology to improve efficiency, and build a workplace culture that encourages growth and success.

One of the greatest strengths of small businesses is their ability to be nimble and adapt quickly. With that agility comes the opportunity to experiment and innovate when it comes to hiring. Rather than being bound by traditional, costly recruitment methods, small businesses have the flexibility to implement creative, cost-effective strategies that work for their unique needs.

As you read through this book, you'll be encouraged to take immediate action. The strategies and resources provided are practical and meant to be applied quickly, allowing you to see results in the short term. I want you to feel empowered to make the decisions that are best for your business and your team, regardless of your budget.

Building a strong, effective team is one of the most valuable investments you can make in your business. When you hire the right people, you create a foundation for growth, innovation, and success. This book will guide you every step of the way, showing you that building your dream team doesn't have to be a luxury reserved for large corporations—it's something any small business can achieve.

Thank you for allowing me to be part of your journey. Let's get started on building the dream team your business deserves!

Chapter 1: The Foundations of Hiring for Small Businesses

Hiring the right team is one of the most crucial steps in building a successful small business. It's not just about finding people to fill open positions—it's about strategically choosing individuals who can help your business grow, thrive, and adapt to changes in the marketplace. This chapter lays the groundwork for effective hiring by helping you understand your business's unique hiring needs and by defining your company culture and values, which will guide your recruitment efforts.

Understanding Your Hiring Needs

Before you post a job listing or start reaching out to potential candidates, it's essential to have a clear understanding of what your business truly needs. This involves identifying the key roles that will drive your business forward and determining the skills necessary to fulfill those roles.

Identifying Key Roles and Skills Essential for Your Business

To build a successful team, you need to pinpoint which roles are critical to your operations. Start by asking yourself the following questions:

- What are the core functions of your business?
- Which tasks are currently being neglected or could be improved?
- Are there gaps in expertise that are holding your business back?
- What skills are necessary to achieve your short-term and long-term goals?

  > Example: Let's say you run a small digital marketing agency. You might identify that while your team is strong in content

> creation, you lack expertise in search engine optimization (SEO). In this case, hiring an SEO specialist would help you enhance your service offerings and attract more clients.

Once you've identified the roles you need to fill, create a list of skills and qualifications that are non-negotiable for each position. For example, if you're hiring a customer support representative, key skills might include excellent communication, problem-solving, and experience with customer service software.

Differentiating Between Full-Time, Part-Time, Freelance, and Remote Workers

Small businesses often have limited budgets, so it's essential to allocate resources wisely when it comes to hiring. Understanding the different types of employment arrangements can help you make cost-effective decisions.

Full-Time Employees:

- Best for core roles that require a consistent presence.

- Ideal for positions that directly impact the growth of your business.
- Offers stability but comes with additional costs like benefits and insurance.

> Example: Hiring a full-time operations manager to oversee daily business activities ensures stability and efficiency.

Part-Time Employees:

- Useful for roles with flexible or fluctuating demands.
- Can help you save on salaries and benefits while still getting essential work done.

> Example: A part-time bookkeeper can manage your finances without the need for a full-time salary.

Freelancers and Contractors:

- Great for short-term projects or specialized skills.
- No need for long-term commitments, which reduces overhead costs.

> Example: If you need a logo designed, hiring a freelance graphic designer is a cost-effective solution.

Remote Workers:

- Expands your talent pool by removing geographical limitations.
- Can reduce office expenses and offer flexibility to employees.

> Example: A remote content writer can produce high-quality articles for your blog from anywhere in the world.

By understanding these different types of workers, you can tailor your hiring strategy to fit your business's needs and budget.

Defining Your Company Culture and Values

Hiring the right talent is not just about skills and experience; it's also about finding individuals who align with your company's culture and values. A strong cultural fit leads to better employee engagement, higher productivity, and lower turnover rates.

How to Attract Candidates Who Align with Your Business Vision

Your company culture is essentially the personality of your business. It's shaped by your mission, values, and the way your team interacts with each other. Here's how to define and communicate your company culture to attract the right candidates:

Clarify Your Mission and Values:

- Clearly articulate what your business stands for and the impact you want to make.
- Incorporate your mission and values into your job descriptions, website, and social media.

> Example: If sustainability is a core value, highlight your commitment to eco-friendly practices in your job postings.

Showcase Your Workplace Environment:

- Use your website and social media channels to showcase your team, work environment, and company events.
- Share testimonials or case studies from current employees about why they enjoy working at your company.

> Example: Post behind-the-scenes photos of team-building activities to give candidates a sense of your work culture.

Offer Unique Perks and Benefits:

Beyond salary, emphasize what makes your workplace special. This could include flexible hours, remote work options, wellness programs, or opportunities for professional development.

> Example: If you offer flexible work schedules, highlight this as a benefit to attract candidates seeking work-life balance.

Creating a Culture Fit Checklist to Screen Applicants

Once you've defined your company culture, the next step is to incorporate it into your hiring process. Creating a culture fit checklist helps you evaluate whether candidates will thrive in your work environment. Here's how to create one:

List Your Core Values:

- Write down 3-5 core values that are essential to your company culture.
- For each value, create specific behaviors or attitudes that align with it.

> Example: If "innovation" is a core value, you might look for candidates who demonstrate creativity, problem-solving skills, and a willingness to take risks.

Craft Culture-Focused Interview Questions:

Ask questions that reveal a candidate's personality, work style, and values.

Use situational and behavioral questions to understand how they've handled past challenges.

Sample Questions:

"Can you give an example of how you've contributed to a team's success in the past?"

"How do you handle disagreements or conflicts with coworkers?"

"What motivates you to do your best work?"

Assess Cultural Alignment in Reference Checks:

- When conducting reference checks, ask previous employers about the candidate's fit within their team.
- Look for feedback related to collaboration, communication, and adaptability.

  > Example: If your company values teamwork, ask the reference about the candidate's ability to work effectively in team settings.

Evaluate for Long-Term Fit:

Consider not just how well a candidate fits your culture today, but also how they will align with your company's future direction.

Look for individuals who are adaptable and willing to grow with your business.

Real-World Examples and Case Studies

Case Study 1: Small Retail Business

A small boutique was struggling to keep up with demand during the holiday season. They decided to hire part-time seasonal staff to manage the influx of customers. By clearly defining their needs (excellent customer service and quick adaptability), they hired two part-time employees who helped increase sales by 20% during the holiday rush.

Case Study 2: Remote Tech Startup

A tech startup needed to scale its development team but had a limited budget. Instead of hiring full-time employees, they opted to bring on freelance developers from around the world. By using platforms like Upwork, they found skilled professionals who could contribute to projects on a flexible, as-needed basis. This approach saved the startup 30% in labor costs compared to hiring locally.

Tips for Small Businesses: Getting Started with Hiring

1. **Leverage Your Network:** Tap into your existing network for referrals. Employees and business partners can recommend candidates who are a good fit.
2. **Start Small**: Begin with one or two critical hires to test your recruitment strategy before scaling up.
3. **Use Technology to Streamline Hiring**: Use free or affordable Applicant Tracking Systems (ATS) like Breezy HR or Zoho Recruit to manage applications and streamline the hiring process.
4. **Offer Trial Periods**: Consider hiring candidates on a probationary or freelance basis to assess their fit before committing to a permanent role.

Conclusion: Laying the Foundation for a Successful Hiring Strategy

Building a dream team for your small business doesn't have to be overwhelming or expensive. By understanding your specific hiring needs, defining a strong company culture, and using strategic recruitment techniques, you can attract top talent without stretching your budget. In the next chapters, we'll explore practical strategies for recruiting, interviewing, onboarding, and retaining employees—all tailored to small business owners who are ready to grow their teams.

Chapter 2: Crafting a Compelling Job Description

In the hiring process, your job description is often the first impression potential candidates have of your business. It's your opportunity to not only attract top talent but also to set clear expectations about the role and your company culture. Crafting an effective job description can make a significant difference in the quality and quantity of applicants you receive, ultimately saving you time and resources in the hiring process. This chapter explores the key elements of creating a compelling job description, highlighting your unique selling points, and leveraging SEO techniques to improve visibility.

Writing Job Descriptions That Attract Top Talent

A job description is more than just a list of duties and qualifications. It's a marketing tool that should appeal to high-quality candidates while accurately reflecting your company's needs and culture. Here are some best practices for writing clear, engaging, and inclusive job descriptions that attract top talent:

Best Practices for Crafting Job Descriptions

Start with a Strong, Descriptive Job Title:

The job title is the first thing candidates see, so it needs to be both descriptive and appealing. Avoid jargon and overly creative titles that may confuse job seekers (e.g., "Marketing Ninja"). Instead, opt for straightforward titles that clearly indicate the role (e.g., "Digital Marketing Specialist").

> Example: Instead of using "Customer Happiness Guru," opt for "Customer Support Representative." This clarity will help you attract the right candidates.

Write an Engaging Introduction:

The opening paragraph should grab the candidate's attention and motivate them to read further. Highlight what makes your company unique, the impact of the role, and why someone would want to join your team.

> Example: "Are you passionate about digital marketing and eager to work in a dynamic startup environment? Join our team at XYZ Agency, where creativity meets innovation, and help us revolutionize the way small businesses connect with their audiences."

Clearly Define Responsibilities and Duties:

Provide a clear and concise list of the role's main responsibilities. Use bullet points to make the information easy to scan. Be specific about what the job entails to help candidates assess if they're a good fit.

Example:

Develop and implement social media strategies to increase brand awareness.

- Create and manage email marketing campaigns to nurture leads.

- Analyze website traffic and user engagement metrics to improve SEO performance.

List the Essential Skills and Qualifications:

Include both "must-have" and "nice-to-have" qualifications. This helps filter out unqualified candidates while encouraging those with the right skill set to apply.

Example:

- Must-Have: 3+ years of experience in digital marketing, proficiency in Google Analytics, strong communication skills.
- Nice-to-Have: Experience with WordPress and Adobe Creative Suite.

Highlight Opportunities for Growth and Development:

Top candidates are often looking for roles that offer growth opportunities. Mention any career advancement, training programs, or mentorship opportunities your company provides.

> Example: "We believe in investing in our team's growth. You'll have access to professional development courses, one-on-one coaching, and the chance to advance into a leadership role."

Focus on Inclusivity and Diversity:

Use inclusive language to attract a diverse pool of candidates. Avoid gender-biased terms and be mindful of phrases that might unintentionally discourage certain groups from applying.

> Example: Instead of "He/She will manage the team," use "The ideal candidate will manage the team." Avoid terms like "rockstar" or "young and energetic," which may deter older applicants.

Include a Compelling Call to Action (CTA):

Encourage candidates to take the next step by including a clear CTA at the end of your job description.

> Example: "Ready to take your marketing career to the next level? Apply today and join our innovative team!"

Common Mistakes to Avoid

- **Being Vague:** Vague job descriptions attract a broad range of applicants, many of whom may not be qualified.
- **Overloading with Requirements:** Listing too many "must-have" qualifications can deter talented candidates who may not meet every single criterion.
- **Neglecting the Company Culture:** Candidates want to know what it's like to work at your company. Make sure to highlight your culture and values.

Highlighting Your Unique Selling Points as an Employer

Small businesses often face stiff competition from larger companies when it comes to attracting top talent. However, small businesses have unique advantages that can appeal to job seekers, especially those looking for meaningful work, flexibility, and a strong sense of community.

How to Showcase Your Small Business's Advantages

Emphasize Your Company's Mission and Impact:

Many candidates are drawn to roles where they can make a meaningful impact. Highlight how employees contribute to your company's mission and the positive effects of their work.

> Example: "At ABC Co., every team member plays a crucial role in helping local businesses thrive. Your work here will directly contribute to our mission of empowering entrepreneurs."

Promote Your Workplace Culture:

Small businesses often offer close-knit work environments where employees can form strong relationships and collaborate closely. Highlight your company's culture, whether it's a family-like atmosphere, a commitment to work-life balance, or a flexible work schedule.

> Example: "Join our friendly, collaborative team where your ideas are valued, and you'll have the flexibility to balance work with your personal life."

Showcase Career Growth Opportunities:

Unlike larger companies where career paths can be rigid, small businesses can offer diverse learning experiences and faster career progression. Emphasize opportunities for employees to take on new challenges and grow within the company.

> Example: "We're a rapidly growing company with plenty of opportunities for advancement. As a member of our team, you'll have the chance to wear multiple hats, develop new skills, and grow into leadership roles."

Highlight Benefits Beyond Salary:

Small businesses might not always be able to compete on salary, but they can offer unique benefits such as flexible hours, remote work options, or extra paid time off.

> Example: "Enjoy a healthy work-life balance with our flexible hours, remote work options, and generous vacation policy."

Leveraging Keywords for Better Job Post Visibility

To attract top talent, it's crucial to ensure your job postings are discoverable. This is where leveraging keywords and search engine optimization (SEO) techniques can help. By optimizing your job descriptions with the right keywords, you can increase visibility on job boards, company career pages, and search engines like Google.

Using SEO to Make Your Job Postings More Discoverable

Research Relevant Keywords:

Start by identifying keywords that job seekers are likely to use when searching for roles similar to yours. Use tools like Google Keyword Planner, Ahrefs, or even LinkedIn job postings for keyword ideas.

Example: If you're hiring a marketing specialist, relevant keywords might include "digital marketing," "SEO specialist," "content marketing," and "social media manager."

Incorporate Keywords Naturally:

Once you have a list of keywords, incorporate them naturally into your job title, job summary, and throughout the job description. Avoid keyword stuffing, which can make your posting look spammy.

> Example: Instead of "We are hiring for a Marketing Guru," use "We are looking for a skilled Digital Marketing Specialist with experience in SEO and content marketing."

Optimize Job Titles for SEO:

Use job titles that are straightforward and aligned with industry standards. This makes it easier for job seekers to find your posting and increases your chances of appearing in search results.

> Example: Instead of a creative title like "Marketing Rockstar," use a more search-friendly title like "Digital Marketing Manager."

Leverage Location-Based Keywords:

If your role requires candidates to work from a specific location, include location-based keywords in your job description. This is especially useful if you're targeting local talent.

> Example: "We are seeking an Office Manager based in Austin, TX, to oversee our day-to-day operations."

Use Job Posting Platforms with Strong SEO:

Platforms like Indeed, LinkedIn, and Glassdoor have strong domain authority and can help boost the visibility of your job postings. Make sure to optimize your listings on these platforms for maximum reach.

Example of an Optimized Job Description

Job Title: Digital Marketing Specialist (Remote)

Job Summary: We are seeking a results-driven Digital Marketing Specialist with experience in SEO, content marketing, and social media management. In this remote role, you'll have the opportunity to shape our digital strategy and drive growth for our clients.

Key Responsibilities:

- Develop and execute digital marketing campaigns across various platforms.
- Conduct keyword research and optimize content for SEO.
- Manage social media channels to increase brand awareness.
- Analyze performance metrics and adjust strategies for maximum ROI.
- Qualifications:

- Bachelor's degree in Marketing or a related field.
- 3+ years of experience in digital marketing.
- Strong knowledge of Google Analytics, SEO best practices, and social media trends.

Perks:

- Fully remote position with flexible hours.
- Opportunities for professional growth and career advancement.
- A supportive and collaborative team culture.

Apply Today: Ready to join our dynamic team? Apply now and take your digital marketing career to the next level!

Conclusion: Crafting Job Descriptions That Stand Out

A well-crafted job description is a powerful tool that can help your small business attract the right candidates. By focusing on clarity, inclusivity, and optimizing for search visibility, you can set your job postings apart from the competition. Remember, your job description is not just a list of tasks—it's a marketing tool that reflects your brand and company culture. Invest time in crafting compelling job descriptions, and you'll see a noticeable improvement in the quality of applicants, ultimately leading to better hires.

By implementing these best practices, highlighting your unique selling points, and leveraging SEO, you can ensure your job postings are seen by top talent who are eager to join your team.

Chapter 3: Cost-Effective Recruitment Strategies

Recruiting the right talent can be a significant challenge for small businesses, especially when operating on a limited budget. However, there are numerous cost-effective strategies that can help you attract top-quality candidates without breaking the bank. This chapter explores actionable ways to leverage free and low-cost job boards, employee referrals, social media, and other affordable recruitment channels to build your dream team. By using these methods, small businesses can compete with larger companies in attracting talent while maintaining a tight budget.

Leveraging Free and Low-Cost Job Boards

Posting job openings on traditional job boards can be costly, but there are many free and low-cost platforms available that offer great exposure. These platforms can help small businesses attract a broad range of candidates without the financial burden.

Top Free and Low-Cost Job Boards

Indeed:

While Indeed offers paid options for boosting your job listing's visibility, it also allows you to post jobs for free. Indeed is one of the most popular job search engines, so even unpaid listings receive a lot of traffic.

> Example: A small bakery looking to hire part-time staff used Indeed's free job posting feature and received over 50 qualified applications within a week.

LinkedIn:

LinkedIn allows you to post a limited number of job openings for free, especially if you have a company page. It's particularly effective for professional and specialized roles, as LinkedIn users are often more engaged in their job searches.

> Example: A tech startup posted a free job listing for a software developer role on LinkedIn and utilized its network to reach out to potential candidates, successfully filling the position without paying for job ads.

Google for Jobs:

Google aggregates job postings from various sources, so optimizing your job listings for Google for Jobs can increase visibility without additional cost. Ensure your job descriptions are well-structured and keyword-optimized.

> Example: An accounting firm saw a 30% increase in applications by optimizing their job postings for Google for Jobs, using relevant keywords and clear job titles.

Craigslist:

Craigslist can be a surprisingly effective platform for certain types of roles, especially in local or service-based industries. The cost is minimal (sometimes free, depending on your location), making it a great option for small businesses.

> Example: A local café posted a job opening on Craigslist for a barista position and was able to fill the role within two days with zero ad spend.

AngelList:

AngelList is ideal for startups looking to hire tech talent. The platform allows you to post job openings for free and reach out to a community of job seekers interested in startup opportunities.

> Example: A new SaaS company used AngelList to find its first marketing manager, leveraging the platform's focus on tech-savvy professionals.

Tips for Maximizing Free Job Boards

- **Optimize Your Job Postings:** Use relevant keywords, a clear job title, and an engaging description to increase the chances of your job posting being discovered.
- **Refresh Your Listings:** Regularly update your job postings to keep them at the top of search results. Some platforms allow you to "bump" your listing to increase visibility.

- **Leverage Niche Job Boards:** Consider using niche job boards specific to your industry (e.g., TechCareers for tech roles or Mediabistro for marketing and media jobs) to attract more targeted candidates.

Networking and Employee Referrals

Networking and employee referrals are among the most cost-effective ways to find quality candidates. They leverage existing connections and can significantly reduce the time and cost associated with recruitment.

Building a Referral Program

A well-structured employee referral program can incentivize your current team to recommend qualified candidates from their networks. Here's how to set up an effective referral program:

Offer Meaningful Incentives:

Monetary rewards are common, but you can also offer extra vacation days, gift cards, or company swag as incentives for successful referrals.

> Example: A marketing agency offered a $500 bonus for any employee whose

referral was hired and stayed with the company for at least six months. This program led to a 20% increase in new hires through referrals.

Promote the Program Internally:

Use internal communication channels like Slack, email newsletters, or team meetings to remind employees about the referral program and the open positions.

> Example: A small IT firm noticed a surge in referrals after holding a monthly "Referral Drive" where employees were encouraged to refer candidates, with a special prize for the most successful referral.

Simplify the Referral Process:

Make it easy for employees to submit referrals by providing a simple online form or even a dedicated email address.

> Example: A restaurant chain streamlined its referral process by creating a Google Form that employees could fill out,

> reducing friction and increasing participation.

Networking at Industry Events

Attending industry events, conferences, and trade shows can also be an effective way to meet potential candidates. Building relationships with professionals in your field can lead to quality hires, especially for niche roles.

- Host Meetups: Consider hosting or sponsoring local meetups relevant to your industry to network with potential candidates in a more informal setting.
- Leverage Professional Associations: Join industry-specific associations where you can network with like-minded professionals and share job openings.

Utilizing Social Media for Recruitment

Social media platforms are powerful tools for reaching a broad audience, including passive job seekers who may not be actively looking for new opportunities. With strategic use, you can attract top talent at little to no cost.

Tips for Finding Talent on LinkedIn, Facebook, and Instagram

LinkedIn: LinkedIn is the go-to platform for professional networking and recruitment. Use LinkedIn's search filters to find candidates with specific skills and experience, and reach out to them directly.

> Example: A graphic design firm used LinkedIn to find freelance designers by posting in industry-specific LinkedIn groups and reaching out to candidates with the right skills.

Facebook: Facebook's vast user base makes it a great platform for reaching a diverse audience. Utilize Facebook Groups, especially those related to your industry, to post job openings.

> Example: A small retail business found its new sales associate by posting in local community Facebook Groups, where members often share job opportunities.

Instagram: Instagram may not be the first platform that comes to mind for recruitment, but it can be highly effective for attracting younger talent, especially for creative roles. Use Instagram Stories, hashtags, and the "Link in Bio" feature to promote job openings.

> Example: A fashion startup used Instagram to showcase its company culture and post job openings in its Stories, attracting candidates who were already fans of the brand.

Creating Engaging Social Media Posts

- Use Eye-Catching Visuals: Include photos or videos that highlight your company culture, team activities, or office space.
- Leverage Hashtags: Use relevant hashtags like #Hiring, #JobOpening, or industry-specific hashtags to increase the reach of your posts.
- Run Social Media Ads: If your budget allows, consider running targeted ads to reach candidates with specific skills or in certain locations.

Hiring Interns and Entry-Level Candidates

Internships and entry-level positions are great ways to bring fresh talent into your business at a lower cost. Developing talent from within can also lead to long-term retention and growth.

Benefits of Hiring Interns

Cost-Effective Talent Pool:

Interns often require lower compensation than full-time employees, making them a budget-friendly option for small businesses.

> Example: A digital marketing agency brought on two interns during the summer, providing them with hands-on experience while benefiting from their contributions to social media and content projects.

Fresh Perspectives:

Interns can bring new ideas and energy to your team, often contributing innovative solutions that more experienced employees might overlook.

> Example: A small tech firm leveraged an intern's expertise in TikTok to launch a new marketing campaign that resulted in

increased brand visibility among younger audiences.

Developing an Internship Program

Define Clear Roles and Responsibilities:

- Ensure that interns have specific projects and tasks to work on, so they gain valuable experience while contributing to your business.

Offer Mentorship Opportunities:

• Pair interns with experienced employees who can guide them, answer their questions, and help them develop their skills.

Evaluate for Future Employment:

- Use internships as a trial period to assess interns' skills, work ethic, and cultural fit. High-performing interns can be offered full-time positions.

Example: A software company converted two of its summer interns into full-time developers, saving on recruitment costs and retaining talent that was already familiar with the company's processes.

Entry-Level Hires as a Cost-Saving Strategy

Hiring entry-level candidates can be a strategic way to build your workforce while keeping costs low. These individuals often bring enthusiasm and a willingness to learn, which can be a valuable asset to your team.

Focus on Potential, Not Just Experience:

- Look for candidates with the right attitude and willingness to learn, even if they lack extensive experience. Invest in training and development to help them grow into the role.

Use Apprenticeship and Training Programs:

- Consider developing in-house training programs to upskill entry-level employees. This investment can pay off in the long run as they become more skilled and take on greater responsibilities.

Example: A boutique marketing agency created an in-house training program for recent graduates, resulting in a pipeline of skilled talent that was promoted to higher positions within the company.

Chapter 4: Interviewing and Assessing Candidates

The interview process is a critical component of hiring, especially for small businesses where every new hire can significantly impact team dynamics and company performance. This chapter explores how to structure effective interviews, assess both hard and soft skills, evaluate cultural fit, and leverage skills assessments. It also covers best practices for virtual interviews, which have become increasingly essential in the era of remote work. By refining your interviewing and assessment techniques, you can make confident, informed hiring decisions that align with your business goals and culture.

Structuring Effective Interviews

A well-structured interview is essential to identify the right candidates. The goal is to ask questions that reveal not only a candidate's skills and experience but also their potential fit within your company.

Crafting Behavioral and Situational Questions

Behavioral Questions focus on past experiences to predict future behavior. These questions help assess how candidates have handled real-life situations in previous roles.

Examples:

- "Tell me about a time when you faced a significant challenge at work. How did you handle it?"
- "Can you give an example of a situation where you had to work under pressure?"
- Purpose: These questions provide insights into a candidate's problem-solving skills, resilience, and ability to manage stress.
- Situational Questions are hypothetical scenarios designed to evaluate how

candidates would handle specific situations relevant to the role.

Examples:

- "If you were leading a project that was falling behind schedule, what steps would you take to get it back on track?"
- "How would you handle a conflict with a coworker over project responsibilities?"
- Purpose: These questions assess critical thinking, decision-making, and adaptability.

Creating a Balanced Interview Structure

Start with an Icebreaker: Begin with a few casual questions to put the candidate at ease. This helps reduce interview jitters and sets a comfortable tone for the conversation.

> Example: "What inspired you to apply for this role at our company?"

Core Competency Questions: Focus on questions that align with the job's key responsibilities.

> Example: For a marketing position, ask, "How do you measure the success of a digital marketing campaign?"

Behavioral and Situational Questions: Integrate both types of questions to get a well-rounded view of the candidate's abilities and mindset.

Cultural Fit Questions: Conclude with questions that explore alignment with your company values.

> Example: "Describe a work environment where you thrive. What aspects are most important to you?"

Best Practices for Interview Structure

- **Create a Consistent Format:** Use the same set of questions for all candidates to ensure a fair comparison.
- **Take Notes:** Document key points from each interview to facilitate the evaluation process.

- **Allocate Time for Candidate Questions**: Encourage candidates to ask questions, which can reveal their interest in the role and company.

Assessing Soft Skills and Cultural Fit

While technical skills are crucial, soft skills and cultural fit often determine long-term success in a role. Small businesses, in particular, rely on cohesive teams where members work well together and share the company's values.

Techniques for Evaluating Communication, Teamwork, and Adaptability

Role-Playing Exercises: Use role-playing scenarios to observe how candidates handle communication in real-time.

> Example: For a customer service role, simulate a difficult customer interaction and ask the candidate to resolve the issue.

Group Interviews: Invite candidates to a group setting to observe their interaction with others, which is especially useful for roles requiring strong teamwork skills.

> Example: For a project management position, ask candidates to collaborate on a mock project to assess their leadership and collaboration skills.

STAR Method: Encourage candidates to use the STAR (Situation, Task, Action, Result) method when answering questions. This helps provide structured and detailed responses, making it easier to evaluate their problem-solving abilities.

> Example: Ask, "Describe a time when you had to adapt to a sudden change at work. What was the outcome?"

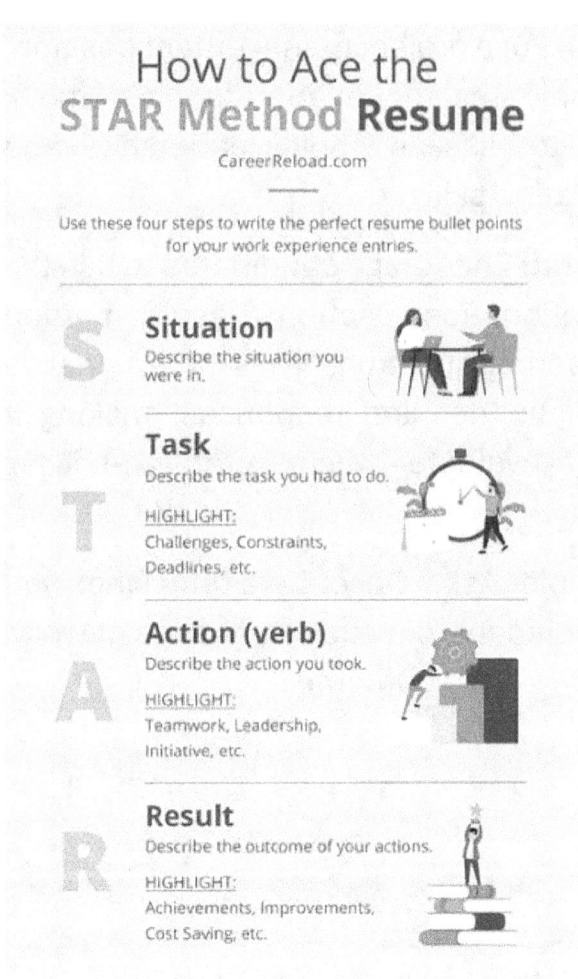

Creating a Culture Fit Checklist

To assess cultural fit, develop a checklist that aligns with your company's values and work environment. This ensures that candidates are evaluated against criteria that reflect your organization's culture.

Sample Culture Fit Checklist:

- Values teamwork and collaboration.
- Shows initiative and problem-solving skills.
- Aligns with our commitment to customer satisfaction.
- Displays a positive attitude and resilience in the face of challenges.

> Example: A tech startup that prioritizes innovation might include "Comfortable with ambiguity and rapid change" as a key cultural fit criterion.

Using Skills Assessments and Trial Projects

Skills assessments and trial projects provide a practical way to evaluate a candidate's abilities beyond what's written on their resume.

Benefits of Skills Assessments

- **Objective Measurement:** Skills assessments offer an objective measure of a candidate's capabilities,

helping to reduce bias in the hiring process.
- **Real-World Relevance:** These tests can be tailored to reflect actual tasks the candidate will encounter in the role.

> Example: A content marketing agency uses writing assessments to gauge a candidate's ability to produce engaging content within a tight deadline.

Types of Assessments to Consider

Technical Tests: For roles that require specific technical skills (e.g., coding, data analysis), create tests that reflect the job's core responsibilities.

> Example: A software development company uses coding challenges to assess programming proficiency.

Practical Assignments: Assign real-world projects that mimic the work the candidate would be doing.

> Example: A graphic design firm asks candidates to create a logo based on a

sample client brief to assess creativity and design skills.

Soft Skills Assessments: Use personality tests and scenario-based questions to evaluate communication, teamwork, and problem-solving abilities.

> Example: A sales team uses role-playing exercises to test negotiation and customer relationship management skills.

Implementing Trial Projects

For key positions, consider a short trial project or probation period where candidates work on actual projects. This allows both the candidate and employer to assess fit before making a long-term commitment.

> Example: A digital marketing firm hires a content strategist on a two-week trial to develop a content calendar, assessing both strategy and execution skills.

Virtual Interviews and Remote Hiring

With remote work becoming increasingly prevalent, virtual interviews have become a standard part of the hiring process. Mastering the art of virtual interviewing can expand your talent pool beyond geographical limitations.

Best Practices for Conducting Video Interviews

Choose the Right Platform: Use reliable video conferencing tools like Zoom, Microsoft Teams, or Google Meet to conduct interviews.

- Tip: Ensure both you and the candidate are familiar with the platform to avoid technical difficulties.

Prepare Candidates in Advance: Send an interview agenda, including the interview format and any technical requirements. This sets clear expectations and helps candidates prepare.

- Example: A consulting firm sends a detailed email with instructions on joining the Zoom call, including a troubleshooting guide for common technical issues.

Test Technology Beforehand: Conduct a test run to ensure your microphone, camera, and internet connection are working properly.

- Tip: Have a backup plan, like a phone number to call in case of technical issues.

Create a Professional Environment: Ensure your background is clutter-free and well-lit. This sets a professional tone and minimizes distractions.

Focus on Engagement: Virtual interviews can feel less personal, so make an effort to build rapport by maintaining eye contact (look into the camera), smiling, and actively listening.

Tips for Assessing Remote Candidates

Ask Remote-Specific Questions:

- "How do you stay productive and motivated when working from home?"
- "Can you give an example of a time you successfully collaborated with a remote team?"

Assess Tech Savviness: Remote roles often require comfort with technology. Consider giving candidates a quick tech challenge, like navigating a new software tool or sharing their screen.

Use Virtual Whiteboards: Tools like Miro or MURAL can be used for collaborative tasks during the interview, such as brainstorming sessions or problem-solving exercises.

> Example: A software company uses a virtual whiteboard to assess a candidate's ability to brainstorm features for a new app, testing both creativity and collaborative skills.

Conducting Group Interviews Remotely

For roles requiring collaboration, consider hosting group interviews on video calls to observe how candidates interact with others in a remote setting.

> Example: A consulting firm uses Zoom breakout rooms to simulate client meetings, allowing candidates to showcase teamwork and leadership in a virtual environment.

Conclusion

Effective interviewing and candidate assessment are crucial steps in building a strong team for your small business. By structuring interviews with a mix of behavioral and situational questions, evaluating both technical and soft skills, and embracing virtual interviewing techniques, you can improve your hiring outcomes. Investing time in the interview process ensures you select candidates who not only have the right skills but also align with your company culture and values, leading to long-term success and growth.

Chapter 5: Onboarding for Success

Onboarding is a critical phase in the hiring process that sets the tone for a new hire's experience and long-term success within your organization. For small businesses, a well-structured onboarding program can lead to increased employee engagement, reduced turnover, and enhanced productivity. This chapter explores strategies to create an engaging onboarding experience, set clear expectations and goals, offer continuous training and development, and leverage mentorship to integrate new hires seamlessly into your team.

Creating an Engaging Onboarding Program

The first few days and weeks of a new hire's journey are crucial for shaping their perception of your company. A positive onboarding experience can significantly impact employee satisfaction and retention rates.

Steps to Ensure New Hires Feel Welcomed and Prepared

Start Before Day One: The onboarding process should begin as soon as a candidate accepts the job offer. This can include sending a welcome email with important information about their first day, providing access to a digital onboarding portal, or mailing a welcome package that includes branded swag or a personalized note.

> Example: A small marketing agency sends new hires a welcome kit that includes a company T-shirt, a branded notebook, and a handwritten welcome note from the CEO. This gesture not only builds excitement but also fosters a sense of belonging before the official start date.

Prepare a Structured Onboarding Plan: Outline the onboarding schedule, including training sessions, team introductions, and meetings. Providing a clear roadmap helps new hires feel more comfortable and reduces the overwhelm that often comes with starting a new job.

> Example: A tech startup uses Trello to create a customized onboarding board for each new employee, listing out tasks, meeting schedules, and key resources. This visual tool helps new hires track their progress and stay organized.

Make Introductions Personal: Arrange one-on-one meetings with key team members and stakeholders. This helps new hires build relationships and understand the company's internal network.

> Example: A small accounting firm schedules virtual coffee chats between new hires and team members from different departments to foster cross-functional collaboration.

Incorporate Company Culture: Share your company's mission, values, and culture during the onboarding process. This can be done through presentations, videos, or interactive sessions. Highlighting your culture early on helps new employees feel aligned with your company's vision.

> Example: An eco-friendly retail brand hosts a "Culture Day" during onboarding, where new hires learn about the company's commitment to sustainability and participate in team-building activities that emphasize their core values.

Onboarding Checklist for Small Businesses

1. Send a welcome email with a detailed first-day agenda.
2. Prepare a workstation (or remote setup) with all necessary tools.
3. Assign a buddy or mentor for new hires.
4. Schedule introductions with team members and leadership.
5. Provide access to digital resources and training materials.

6. Conduct a tour (virtual or in-person) of the office environment.
7. Schedule check-ins at the end of the first week and first month.

Setting Clear Expectations and Goals

One of the biggest challenges for new hires is understanding what is expected of them. Clear communication of expectations and performance metrics can set the stage for long-term success.

How to Establish KPIs and Performance Metrics from Day One

Define Key Performance Indicators (KPIs): Identify specific, measurable goals that align with your business objectives. These should be communicated during the onboarding process so that new hires know exactly what they need to achieve.

> Example: A digital marketing agency sets a KPI for a new social media manager to increase Instagram engagement by 20% within the first 90 days. This provides a clear target for the employee to aim for.

Set SMART Goals: Ensure that the goals are Specific, Measurable, Achievable, Relevant, and Time-bound. This framework helps new employees focus on what matters most.

> Example: For a sales representative, a SMART goal might be: "Close 10 new client contracts worth at least $5,000 each within the first quarter."

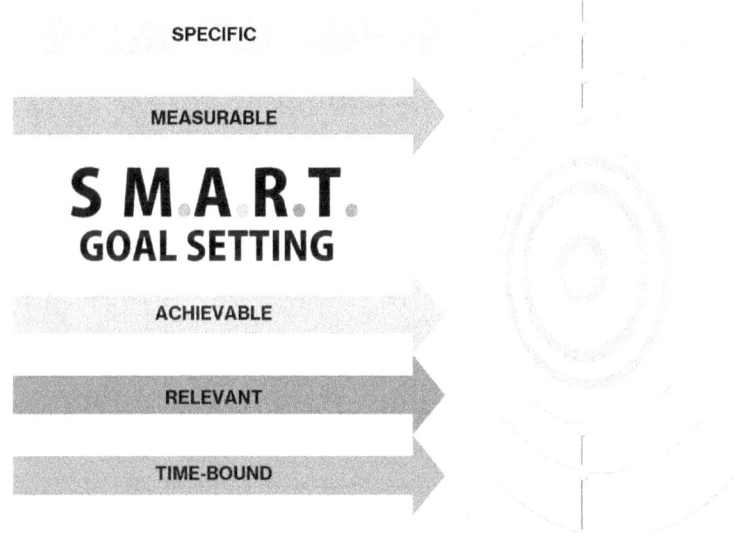

Regular Check-Ins and Feedback: Schedule weekly or bi-weekly check-ins during the initial months to assess progress and provide feedback. This not only helps new hires stay on track but also fosters open communication.

Example: A small software company uses a 30-60-90 day plan, where new hires are evaluated at each milestone to ensure they are meeting their goals and adjusting as needed.

Tools for Tracking Performance

- **Project Management Software:** Tools like Asana, Monday.com, or Trello can help track progress on tasks and projects.
- **Performance Review Platforms:** Software like Lattice or 15Five allows for continuous feedback and performance assessments.
- **Scorecards:** Create a simple scorecard that tracks KPIs and accomplishments, which can be reviewed during one-on-one meetings.

Providing Continuous Training and Development

Investing in employee development is essential, especially for small businesses that rely on a lean but highly skilled team. Continuous training not only boosts employee morale but also improves productivity and retention.

Budget-Friendly Options for Skill-Building and Career Growth

Online Learning Platforms: Encourage employees to leverage platforms like EBL Training, LinkedIn Learning, Udemy, or Coursera. Many courses are affordable, and some offer certifications that can enhance the employee's skill set.

> Example: A boutique design agency provides access to a Udemy course on advanced Adobe Photoshop techniques, allowing their graphic designers to upskill at their own pace.

In-House Training: Leverage the expertise within your team by conducting internal workshops or lunch-and-learn sessions. This not only saves costs but also promotes knowledge sharing.

> Example: A small law firm schedules monthly lunch-and-learn sessions where senior partners share insights on industry trends and case management.

Mentorship Programs: Pair new hires with experienced employees to provide guidance and support. This helps in faster learning and smoother integration into the company culture.

> Example: An e-commerce startup assigns a "learning buddy" to each new hire, ensuring they have someone to turn to for questions during their first few months.

Encourage Continuous Improvement: Create a culture of lifelong learning by setting aside a budget for professional development, even if it's modest. Encourage employees to attend industry webinars, workshops, or conferences.

> Example: A wellness center allocates a small budget for their trainers to attend annual fitness conventions, which keeps them updated on the latest trends in the industry.

Using Technology for Training

- Learning Management Systems (LMS): Implement LMS platforms like TalentLMS or Thinkific to centralize training resources and track employee progress.
- Gamification: Use gamified elements like quizzes and badges to make learning more engaging.

> Example: A tech company uses gamification in their onboarding process, where new hires earn badges for completing different training modules, making the experience interactive and fun.

The Role of Mentorship in Employee Success

Mentorship can significantly accelerate a new hire's integration and performance. For small businesses, a strong mentorship program can be a cost-effective way to develop talent and improve retention.

Pairing New Hires with Experienced Team Members for Faster Integration

The Benefits of Mentorship: Mentors can provide valuable insights, answer questions, and offer support that goes beyond formal training. This helps new hires navigate the company's culture and processes more effectively.

> Example: A small PR firm pairs each new account executive with a senior account manager who guides them through the nuances of client communication and project management.

Mentor-Mentee Matching: To maximize the effectiveness of the mentorship program, pair new hires with mentors who have similar professional interests or backgrounds.

> Example: A nonprofit organization pairs new program coordinators with experienced grant writers to help them understand the intricacies of fundraising.

Setting Clear Expectations for Mentorship: Define the goals of the mentorship program, such as helping new hires ramp up faster or preparing them for leadership roles. Regularly check in to assess the mentorship's progress and effectiveness.

Creating a Mentorship Framework

1. Kickoff Meeting: Arrange an initial meeting between the mentor and mentee to establish rapport and set expectations.
2. Regular Check-Ins: Schedule bi-weekly or monthly meetings to discuss progress, challenges, and career development.
3. Feedback Loop: Encourage mentors to provide constructive feedback and recognize mentees' achievements.

> Example: A tech startup uses quarterly feedback sessions to assess the success of their mentorship program, making adjustments as needed based on

feedback from both mentors and mentees.

Mentorship Case Study

A small digital marketing agency noticed high turnover among new hires due to a steep learning curve. To address this, they implemented a mentorship program where senior marketers mentored new team members for their first six months. This program resulted in a 30% increase in retention rates and faster onboarding times, allowing new employees to contribute to client projects more quickly.

Conclusion

A well-executed onboarding process goes beyond paperwork and orientation. By creating an engaging onboarding experience, setting clear expectations, providing continuous training, and leveraging mentorship, small businesses can set their new hires up for long-term success. The investment in a structured onboarding program not only improves employee satisfaction and retention but also boosts overall company performance.

Chapter 6: Leveraging Freelancers and Remote Workers

The modern workforce is rapidly evolving, and small businesses are increasingly turning to freelancers and remote workers to fill critical skill gaps, reduce overhead costs, and scale their operations. Leveraging this flexible talent pool can be a game-changer for small businesses looking to remain competitive in a dynamic market. This chapter delves into the benefits of hiring freelancers, how to find and vet quality candidates, strategies for managing remote teams, and the legal considerations when choosing between contract workers and full-time employees.

Benefits of Hiring Freelancers

Freelancers offer numerous advantages, especially for small businesses that need flexibility in staffing and access to specialized skills without the long-term commitment of full-time employees.

Flexibility and Scalability

On-Demand Talent: Freelancers provide the flexibility to scale your workforce up or down based on your business needs. This is especially useful for project-based work, seasonal demands, or when your business is experiencing rapid growth.

> Example: A small e-commerce business that sees a spike in sales during the holiday season can hire freelance graphic designers and copywriters to handle increased marketing efforts, then scale back after the busy period.

Diverse Skill Sets: Freelancers often bring specialized skills and experience that may not be available in-house. Whether it's SEO optimization, graphic design, or content creation, freelancers can fill these gaps quickly.

> Example: A startup that needs a mobile app developed can hire a freelance app developer with niche expertise in a specific programming language, rather than training an in-house team from scratch.

Cost Savings

Lower Overhead: Hiring freelancers can reduce costs associated with full-time employees, such as benefits, taxes, and office space. This can be particularly beneficial for small businesses with tight budgets.

> Example: A boutique marketing firm can save on overhead by hiring freelance social media managers who work remotely, eliminating the need for additional office space and equipment.

Pay Per Project: Freelancers are typically paid on a per-project basis, which allows you to control costs and allocate your budget more effectively. There's no need to commit to a long-term salary if you only need assistance for a few months.

> Example: A local restaurant launching a new website can hire a freelance web developer for the project duration, avoiding the cost of a full-time web developer.

Access to Global Talent

Remote Work Opportunities: The rise of remote work means you can hire freelancers from anywhere in the world, giving you access to a broader talent pool. This can be especially useful for specialized skills that may be scarce in your local market.

> Example: A tech company based in a small town can hire a freelance cybersecurity expert from another country, ensuring access to top talent without geographical constraints.

Finding and Vetting Freelancers

With so many freelancers available online, finding the right fit for your business can be challenging. However, using the right platforms and having a thorough vetting process in place can help you source high-quality talent.

Best Platforms to Source Quality Freelancers

Upwork: One of the largest freelancing platforms, Upwork offers a wide range of freelancers across various industries. You can post job listings, review proposals, and select candidates based on their ratings and portfolio.

> Example: A SaaS company looking for a freelance technical writer can post a job on Upwork, receive proposals, and select a candidate based on their previous work samples and client reviews.

Fiverr: Known for its quick turnaround and budget-friendly options, Fiverr is ideal for smaller projects. You can hire freelancers for specific tasks like logo design, video editing, or social media content creation.

> Example: A small bakery needing a new logo can find a graphic designer on Fiverr who can deliver high-quality designs within a few days for a reasonable price.

LinkedIn: For professional freelancers with niche expertise, LinkedIn is an excellent platform. You can use LinkedIn's search features to find freelancers, check their recommendations, and connect directly.

> Example: A law firm needing specialized legal content can use LinkedIn to find freelance legal writers with the right industry experience.

Tips for Vetting Freelancers

Check Portfolios and Samples: Always review a freelancer's portfolio to assess the quality of their previous work. Ask for samples relevant to your project to ensure they have the experience needed.

> Example: A small business looking for a freelance SEO specialist can request case studies or examples of previous successful SEO campaigns.

Conduct Interviews: Treat the hiring process for freelancers like you would for full-time employees. Schedule a video interview to discuss their experience, approach to the project, and communication style.

> Example: An online retailer interviewing a freelance digital marketer can use the interview to gauge their familiarity with platforms like Google Ads and Facebook Ads.

Start with a Test Project: Before committing to a long-term contract, consider starting with a smaller, paid test project to evaluate the freelancer's skills, reliability, and work ethic.

> Example: A nonprofit organization hiring a freelance grant writer can start with a small grant application to see if the

> freelancer can deliver high-quality work within deadlines.

Managing Remote Teams Effectively

Hiring freelancers and remote workers offers flexibility but also presents unique challenges in terms of communication, collaboration, and productivity. Implementing effective management strategies is crucial for getting the most out of your remote team.

Tools and Strategies for Keeping Remote Workers Productive

Project Management Tools: Platforms like Trello, Asana, and Monday.com help keep tasks organized and ensure everyone is on the same page. Use these tools to assign tasks, set deadlines, and track progress.

> Example: A digital marketing agency uses Asana to manage a team of freelance content writers, ensuring that each article is assigned, reviewed, and published on schedule.

Communication Platforms: Tools like Slack, Microsoft Teams, and Zoom facilitate real-time communication, making it easier to stay connected with remote workers. Establishing a dedicated channel for quick updates can help streamline communication.

> Example: A small software company with remote developers uses Slack for daily stand-ups and Zoom for weekly team meetings to maintain clear communication.

Time Tracking and Productivity Tools: Platforms like Toggl and Hubstaff can help you monitor the hours your freelancers and remote workers are putting in, ensuring transparency and accountability.

> Example: A design studio uses Hubstaff to track the time their freelance graphic designers spend on each project, ensuring accurate billing.

Set Clear Expectations and Goals: Clearly outline project timelines, deliverables, and communication expectations. Having well-documented processes can help remote workers understand their responsibilities.

> Example: A consultancy firm provides a detailed project brief and timeline for each freelancer, setting clear expectations for deliverables and deadlines.

Contract Workers vs. Full-Time Employees

When deciding between hiring contract workers and full-time employees, small businesses need to consider the legal and financial implications. Both options have their advantages, and the choice largely depends on your business needs, budget, and long-term goals.

Legal Considerations

Employment Laws: Full-time employees are entitled to benefits like health insurance, retirement plans, and paid time off, whereas freelancers and contract workers are typically responsible for their own taxes and benefits. It's important to classify workers correctly to avoid legal issues.

> Example: A small graphic design firm hires freelancers for specific projects and ensures they sign independent contractor agreements to clarify their non-employee status.

Intellectual Property: Protect your business by including clauses in your contracts regarding the ownership of work produced by freelancers. This ensures that all intellectual property rights are transferred to your company.

> Example: A tech startup working with freelance software developers includes an IP assignment clause in their contracts to secure ownership of the code.

Best Use Cases for Each Type of Worker

Contract Workers: Ideal for project-based work, seasonal spikes, or specialized skills that are not needed on a full-time basis.

> Example: An events management company hires contract photographers and videographers for coverage during

> peak wedding seasons, reducing costs during off-seasons.

Full-Time Employees: Best for roles that require consistent output, deep company knowledge, or positions that align with long-term strategic goals.

> Example: A growing small business hires a full-time marketing manager to develop and execute comprehensive marketing strategies, ensuring continuity and brand alignment.

Cost Comparison: Contract vs. Full-Time

- **Freelancer Rates:** While freelancers may charge higher hourly rates, you save on benefits, office space, and long-term commitments.
- **Full-Time Salaries:** Employees may come at a lower hourly cost but include added expenses such as healthcare, retirement contributions, and paid leave.

Example: A startup that needs occasional PR support finds it more cost-effective to hire a freelance public relations consultant at $100/hour rather than a full-time employee with a $60,000 annual salary plus benefits.

Conclusion

Leveraging freelancers and remote workers offers small businesses a flexible, cost-effective way to access top talent and scale operations. By understanding the benefits, knowing where to find quality freelancers, implementing effective management strategies, and being aware of the legal implications, you can build a successful hybrid workforce that meets your business needs.

Chapter 7: Employee Retention on a Budget

Retaining top talent is one of the most significant challenges small businesses face. High turnover rates can be costly, not just in terms of recruiting and training expenses but also in lost productivity and employee morale. However, retaining employees doesn't always require big budgets or lavish perks. This chapter will explore strategies for improving employee retention on a budget, focusing on building a positive work environment, offering non-monetary benefits, recognizing performance, and providing career development opportunities.

Building a Positive Work Environment

Creating a positive work environment is crucial for employee retention. When employees feel valued, respected, and part of a supportive culture, they are more likely to stay with your company long-term. While competitive salaries are important, fostering a culture that prioritizes well-being and engagement can significantly impact retention rates without requiring substantial financial investments.

Fostering a Collaborative and Inclusive Culture

Encourage Open Communication:

Implementing open-door policies where employees feel comfortable sharing their ideas, concerns, and feedback can help create a sense of belonging and trust. Regularly scheduled team meetings, town halls, and anonymous feedback surveys are effective ways to maintain open lines of communication.

> Example: A small marketing agency holds monthly town hall meetings where employees can discuss challenges, propose new ideas, and celebrate team

achievements. This openness fosters a culture of collaboration and innovation.

Promote Team Building Activities: Team-building activities, both virtual and in-person, can help employees bond and improve their working relationships. Activities like brainstorming sessions, problem-solving challenges, or social events like virtual happy hours can strengthen the team dynamic.

> Example: A remote-first software company organizes monthly virtual game nights where team members can unwind and socialize, helping to build camaraderie among distributed employees.

Show Appreciation: Sometimes, a simple thank-you note, a shout-out in a meeting, or recognizing someone's hard work on the company's social media can go a long way in making employees feel valued.

> Example: A local retail store has a "Star of the Month" program, where they feature a

> top-performing employee on their social media accounts, highlighting their contributions to the team.

Creating a Supportive Work-Life Balance

Flexible Scheduling: Offering flexible working hours can significantly improve job satisfaction. Allowing employees to adjust their schedules to accommodate personal commitments shows that you value their work-life balance.

> Example: A small accounting firm offers flexible working hours during tax season, allowing employees to start earlier or later to accommodate family responsibilities.

Promote Wellness Initiatives: Investing in wellness programs doesn't have to be expensive. You can organize wellness challenges, provide access to online fitness classes, or encourage mindfulness breaks during the day.

> Example: A small tech startup encourages employees to take a daily "wellness break," where they can meditate, stretch,

> or go for a walk. This initiative has led to increased productivity and reduced stress levels.

Offering Non-Monetary Perks and Benefits

While salary is a significant factor in employee satisfaction, non-monetary perks can be just as important in retaining talent, especially for small businesses that may not have the budget to offer high salaries. By offering creative, non-financial benefits, you can keep employees happy and engaged.

Affordable Perks to Boost Employee Satisfaction

Remote Work Options: The flexibility to work from home, even part-time, can be a huge draw for employees. Remote work saves employees commuting time and costs, leading to higher job satisfaction.

> Example: A consulting firm allows its employees to work remotely on Fridays, giving them a head start on the weekend and reducing burnout.

Flexible Paid Time Off (PTO): Instead of the traditional model of separate vacation, sick, and personal days, offer a combined PTO policy. This flexibility empowers employees to take time off when they need it, promoting a healthier work-life balance.

> Example: A digital marketing agency switched to an unlimited PTO policy, trusting employees to manage their time effectively. This change has resulted in increased morale and retention.

Casual Dress Code: Allowing employees to dress comfortably at work, especially in non-customer-facing roles, can increase job satisfaction and reduce stress.

> Example: A software development firm with a casual dress policy noticed a boost in employee morale as team members felt more comfortable and relaxed at work.

Recognition Programs that Don't Break the Bank

Employee of the Month: Recognizing one standout employee each month can be an effective and inexpensive way to boost morale. Offer small incentives like a gift card, preferred parking spot, or a featured mention in the company newsletter.

> Example: A small healthcare clinic uses a peer-nominated Employee of the Month program to recognize hard-working staff, increasing team engagement and motivation.

Experience-Based Rewards: Instead of offering cash bonuses, consider experience-based rewards like a half-day off, a wellness gift basket, or a subscription to an online learning platform.

> Example: A small design studio rewards high-performing employees with free access to an online course of their choice, encouraging both personal and professional growth.

Recognizing and Rewarding Performance

Acknowledging employees for their hard work is essential for motivation and retention. You don't 'need a big budget to show appreciation; sometimes, the most meaningful rewards are personalized and thoughtful.

Implementing Low-Cost Recognition Programs

Peer-to-Peer Recognition: Create opportunities for employees to recognize each other's efforts. Tools like Bonusly, Slack's'recognition channels, or even a simple bulletin board where team members can post notes of appreciation can foster a supportive work environment.

> Example: A small IT company uses a Slack channel where team members can give "k"dos" "o colleagues for going above and beyond. This public recognition boosts morale and encourages a positive culture.

Monthly or Quarterly Awards: Recognize teams or individuals who have made significant contributions over a period. These awards don't have to be costly—consider offering certificates, plaques, or even a "trophy" that circulates among winners.

> Example: A small nonprofit awards a "Service Excellence" "Trophy to the department that exceeded its goals for the quarter". The trophy comes with bragging rights and a group lunch with the executive director.

Low-Cost Incentives for Motivation

Personalized Rewards: Offer low-cost rewards that are meaningful to your employees, such as gift cards to their favorite coffee shop, books on their wish list, or personalized thank-you notes.

> Example: A small publishing company has a tradition where employees receive personalized, handwritten thank-you notes from the CEO for completing challenging projects.

Employee Appreciation Events: Hosting appreciation events like potlucks, game nights, or themed office days can help boost morale without a hefty price tag.

> Example: An insurance agency organizes quarterly potlucks where team members

> share homemade dishes, fostering a sense of community and appreciation.

Career Development and Promotion Opportunities

One of the most effective ways to retain employees is to invest in their growth and development. Providing career development opportunities shows employees that you value their future and want to help them achieve their career goals.

Providing Growth Paths to Retain Top Talent

Create Individual Development Plans (IDPs): Work with employees to develop personalized growth plans that align with their career aspirations and your company's goals. IDPs can include a mix of formal training, mentorship, and stretch assignments.

> Example: A small engineering firm creates IDPs for junior engineers, outlining a clear path to senior roles within five years. This transparency has helped reduce turnover among early-career employees.

Offer Internal Promotions and Lateral Moves: Encourage employees to take on new challenges within your organization by promoting from within or allowing lateral moves to different departments.

> Example: A boutique PR agency fills 80% of its managerial positions through internal promotions, fostering a culture of growth and loyalty.

Budget-Friendly Training and Development Programs

Online Learning Resources: Leverage free or low-cost online platforms like [EBL Training](), Coursera, Udemy, or LinkedIn Learning to provide training and upskilling opportunities. These platforms offer courses on various topics, allowing employees to enhance their skills at their own pace.

> Example: A small retail business partners with Udemy to provide free access to courses on leadership and customer service, leading to improved team performance and satisfaction.

Mentorship Programs: Pairing new hires with experienced employees can accelerate onboarding, build relationships, and provide ongoing support.

> Example: A small legal firm assigns each new paralegal a senior attorney as a mentor, helping them navigate the complexities of legal work and grow their skills.

Encouraging Continuous Learning

Lunch and Learn Sessions: Organize informal training sessions where employees can learn new skills over lunch. Topics can range from industry trends to personal development.

> Example: A small architecture firm hosts monthly Lunch and Learn sessions where employees present case studies of their recent projects, encouraging knowledge sharing.

Job Rotation Programs: Allow employees to rotate between different roles or departments to broaden their skills and experience. This can also help you identify employees' strengths and areas for development.

> Example: A family-owned restaurant rotates staff between kitchen, service, and management roles, helping them develop a holistic understanding of the business.

Conclusion

Employee retention doesn't have to be expensive. By fostering a positive work environment, offering meaningful non-monetary perks, recognizing performance, and providing opportunities for growth and development, small businesses can retain top talent even on a limited budget. Implementing these strategies not only boosts morale and engagement but also helps create a loyal workforce that is committed to the long-term success of your company.

Chapter 8: Legal and Compliance Considerations

Navigating the legal and compliance landscape is crucial for small businesses, especially when it comes to hiring and managing employees. Mistakes in this area can lead to costly penalties, legal disputes, and reputational damage. This chapter will explore the essential legal and compliance considerations for small businesses, including understanding employment laws, avoiding discrimination in hiring, correctly classifying workers, and maintaining accurate HR documentation. By following these guidelines, you can protect your business while fostering a fair and compliant workplace.

Understanding Employment Laws

Hiring employees involves more than just finding the right talent; it also requires adherence to various employment laws that govern hiring practices, employee contracts, wages, and more. Small businesses must ensure compliance with both federal and state laws to avoid legal pitfalls.

Navigating the Basics of Hiring Laws

Fair Labor Standards Act (FLSA): The FLSA establishes minimum wage, overtime pay, recordkeeping, and youth employment standards. As of 2024, the federal minimum wage is $7.25 per hour, but many states have set higher minimum wages. Employers must also pay non-exempt employees overtime at a rate of 1.5 times their regular pay for hours worked over 40 in a week.

> Example: A small restaurant in California needs to comply with the state's minimum wage of $15.50 per hour, which is higher than the federal minimum. Failure to do so could result in hefty fines and back pay to employees.

Family and Medical Leave Act (FMLA): The FMLA entitles eligible employees to up to 12 weeks of unpaid, job-protected leave per year for specific family and medical reasons. Small businesses with 50 or more employees must comply with FMLA requirements.

> Example: A tech startup with 55 employees ensures that its HR policies

> include provisions for FMLA leave, allowing employees to take time off for childbirth, adoption, or serious health conditions.

Equal Employment Opportunity (EEO):

Employers must comply with EEO laws, which prohibit discrimination based on race, color, religion, sex, national origin, age, disability, or genetic information.

> Example: A small construction company ensures that its job advertisements and interview processes are free from discriminatory language, thereby promoting a diverse and inclusive workforce.

Drafting Employment Contracts

At-Will Employment: In many states, employees are considered "at-will," meaning they can be terminated at any time for any lawful reason. However, it's essential to clarify this in employment contracts to avoid wrongful termination claims.

> Example: A marketing firm includes an "at-will" clause in its employment contracts to protect itself from potential lawsuits if it needs to terminate an employee's contract unexpectedly.

Non-Disclosure Agreements (NDAs): NDAs protect sensitive business information. Small businesses should require employees to sign NDAs, especially if they handle proprietary information.

> Example: A small R&D firm includes an NDA in its onboarding process to prevent employees from sharing trade secrets with competitors.

Avoiding Discrimination in Hiring

Ensuring a fair and inclusive hiring process is not only the right thing to do but also a legal requirement. Discrimination in hiring can lead to lawsuits, fines, and damage to your company's reputation.

Best Practices for Fair and Inclusive Recruitment

Crafting Inclusive Job Descriptions: Use gender-neutral language and focus on the skills and qualifications required for the job, rather than personal characteristics. Avoid using biased terms that may discourage certain groups from applying.

> Example: Instead of stating, "Looking for a young, energetic salesperson," a retail company updates its job posting to, "Seeking a dynamic salesperson with excellent customer service skills."

Implementing Structured Interviews: Structured interviews, where each candidate is asked the same set of questions, can help reduce bias and ensure a fair evaluation process.

> Example: A small software company uses a standardized set of behavioral interview questions to assess candidates' problem-solving and teamwork skills, which helps minimize unconscious bias in hiring.

Training Hiring Managers on EEO Laws: Regular training on anti-discrimination laws can help hiring managers make fair and legal hiring decisions.

> Example: A nonprofit organization conducts annual training sessions for its hiring managers on diversity and inclusion, ensuring compliance with EEO regulations.

Avoiding Discriminatory Practices

Blind Recruitment: Removing identifying information, such as names and addresses, from resumes can help reduce bias and promote a more diverse candidate pool.

> Example: An accounting firm implements blind recruitment practices to increase diversity among its applicants, resulting in a more inclusive workforce.

Accommodation for Disabilities: The Americans with Disabilities Act (ADA) requires employers to provide reasonable accommodations for employees with disabilities.

> Example: A small manufacturing company ensures its office space is wheelchair accessible and provides assistive technology for visually impaired employees.

Classifying Workers Correctly

Misclassifying workers as independent contractors instead of employees can lead to legal and financial repercussions, including back taxes, penalties, and lawsuits. It's essential to understand the differences between employees and independent contractors to ensure compliance with labor laws.

Distinguishing Between Employees and Independent Contractors

The ABC Test: Many states use the ABC test to determine worker classification. To be classified as an independent contractor, the worker must be free from control, perform work outside the usual course of the business, and be engaged in an independently established trade.

> Example: A graphic design company hires a freelance designer for a one-time project. Since the designer works independently and offers services to multiple clients, they qualify as an independent contractor.

IRS 20-Factor Test: The IRS uses a 20-factor test to assess whether a worker is an employee or an independent contractor. Factors include the level of control over the work, the worker's investment in equipment, and the opportunity for profit or loss.

> Example: A small catering business hires part-time staff for events. Since the business controls their schedule, provides equipment, and pays an hourly wage, the workers are classified as employees.

Penalties for Misclassification

Financial Consequences: Misclassifying employees as contractors can result in back taxes, penalties, and interest. Additionally, employers may be liable for unpaid benefits, such as health insurance and retirement contributions.

> Example: A startup faced a $50,000 fine after incorrectly classifying its marketing team as independent contractors, leading to a costly audit.

Keeping Up with HR Documentation

Proper HR documentation is critical for compliance and protecting your business from potential legal disputes. Keeping accurate records ensures that your business is prepared for audits, legal challenges, and other compliance issues.

Essential Forms and Records for Small Business Hiring

Employee Personnel Files: These should include job applications, resumes, offer letters, signed employee handbooks, and performance reviews. It's essential to keep these files secure and confidential.

> Example: A dental practice maintains digital personnel files using HR software,

making it easy to access records while ensuring data security.

Form I-9 for Employment Eligibility: All employers in the U.S. must verify the identity and employment eligibility of new hires using Form I-9. Failure to comply can result in fines.

> Example: A small retail shop uses an electronic I-9 compliance system to streamline the verification process and ensure compliance with immigration laws.

W-4 and Payroll Records: Employers must collect Form W-4 from employees to determine tax withholding. Additionally, maintaining accurate payroll records is crucial for compliance with wage and hour laws.

> Example: A small construction company uses a payroll software solution to manage employee tax withholdings and ensure timely wage payments.

Implementing Document Retention Policies

Compliance with Recordkeeping Requirements: The Fair Labor Standards Act (FLSA) requires employers to retain payroll records for at least three years. Personnel files, including disciplinary records, should be kept for a minimum of one year after termination.

> Example: A law firm sets up a document retention schedule to ensure compliance with legal requirements, preventing potential fines during audits.

Secure Storage of Sensitive Information: Protect sensitive employee information by using secure digital storage solutions or locked physical filing cabinets. Only authorized personnel should have access to these records.

> Example: A healthcare clinic uses encrypted cloud storage to keep employee health records confidential and secure, complying with the Health Insurance Portability and Accountability Act (HIPAA).

Navigating Audits and Legal Requests

Being Prepared for Audits: Ensure that your HR documentation is up-to-date and readily available in case of audits by government agencies like the Department of Labor or the IRS.

> Example: A small logistics company conducts quarterly internal audits of its HR files to ensure compliance with labor laws and prepare for potential government audits.

Responding to Legal Requests: If your business is involved in a legal dispute, having accurate and well-organized HR documentation can support your case.

> Example: A small manufacturing firm was able to avoid a wrongful termination lawsuit by presenting thorough documentation of the employee's performance issues and disciplinary actions.

Conclusion

Legal and compliance considerations are crucial for small businesses looking to build a strong, compliant workforce. By understanding employment laws, promoting fair hiring practices, correctly classifying workers, and maintaining accurate HR documentation, you can protect your business from costly legal issues and foster a positive work environment. Implementing these best practices not only ensures compliance but also contributes to long-term business success.

Chapter 9: Scaling Your Team as Your Business Grows

As a small business grows, one of the most challenging yet critical aspects of maintaining success is scaling the team. Scaling involves knowing when to hire, how to manage fluctuating workloads, building a reliable talent pipeline, and deciding between outsourcing and in-house hiring. Each of these decisions can significantly impact the long-term health and efficiency of your business. In this chapter, we will explore the strategies and best practices for scaling your team, offering insights into recognizing when to hire, planning for seasonal and project-based hiring, building a talent pipeline, and choosing between outsourcing and in-house hiring.

Knowing When to Hire

Hiring is a critical decision that often comes with significant financial and organizational implications. However, knowing when to hire is just as important as knowing who to hire. Understanding the signs that it's time to expand your team is essential for sustainable growth and operational efficiency.

Signs That It's Time to Expand Your Team

Overwhelmed Staff: One of the most obvious signs that it's time to hire is when your current team is stretched thin and unable to keep up with the workload. If key employees are frequently staying late, experiencing burnout, or failing to meet deadlines, it's likely a signal that additional help is needed.

> Example: A small e-commerce business experiences a surge in sales due to a viral social media campaign. The team's customer service representatives are overwhelmed with inquiries, and order

fulfillment is delayed. Recognizing the pressure, the business owner hires two additional customer support agents to handle the influx of orders, allowing the current team to focus on growth.

Declining Customer Satisfaction: If your customers begin to experience delays in receiving services or products or notice a decrease in quality, it's a clear indicator that the business is understaffed. Hiring additional team members can help maintain or improve service levels and keep your customers satisfied.

> Example: A software-as-a-service (SaaS) company begins receiving complaints about slow response times from the technical support team. The manager realizes that their support team, though efficient, is too small to handle the growing number of users. They decide to expand the team by hiring more support agents to ensure that issues are resolved quickly.

New Opportunities or Product Launches: If your business is expanding into new markets, launching new products, or creating new services, you may need to hire employees with specialized skills to manage these changes. Hiring before the demand arises can ensure that your business is prepared to seize opportunities quickly.

> Example: A digital marketing agency is branching out into SEO services. The current team lacks expertise in this area, so the agency decides to hire an experienced SEO specialist to handle new client requests. This allows the agency to deliver top-quality service without missing a beat.

Inability to Focus on Growth: If you, as the business owner or manager, find yourself bogged down by routine tasks that prevent you from focusing on growth strategies, it's time to hire. Hiring new talent can free up your time to focus on scaling your business.

> Example: A small retail store owner spends most of her time managing

> inventory and handling customer complaints. As sales grow, she realizes she is not dedicating enough time to expanding the product line or marketing the business. She hires a store manager to handle day-to-day operations, freeing herself to focus on growth.

High Employee Turnover: High turnover rates can signal that your employees are overwhelmed or unhappy with their workload. If employees are leaving due to burnout or frustration, hiring additional team members can help alleviate pressure and improve morale.

> Example: A startup in the tech industry is struggling with high turnover rates. Employees are working long hours to meet project deadlines, leading to burnout. The company decides to hire more engineers to distribute the workload, which helps reduce stress and improve employee retention.

Planning for Seasonal and Project-Based Hiring

Many businesses experience fluctuations in their workload based on the time of year, upcoming projects, or product launches. Understanding how to plan for these seasonal or project-based hiring needs can help businesses manage fluctuating workloads without overwhelming their permanent staff or overstretching their budgets.

Strategies for Managing Fluctuating Workloads

Analyze Historical Data: One of the first steps in planning for seasonal or project-based hiring is analyzing historical data to identify trends in workload fluctuations. By examining past years, you can predict when you will need additional staff and how many people you should hire.

> Example: A seasonal garden center analyzes past sales and customer traffic patterns and determines that they need to hire additional salespeople and cashiers for the spring planting season. They use

> this data to plan ahead and hire seasonal workers three months in advance.

Hire Temporary or Seasonal Workers: Temporary or seasonal workers can provide the flexibility you need to handle increased demand during peak periods without the long-term commitment of hiring full-time employees. This approach is particularly useful in industries like retail, hospitality, and agriculture.

> Example: A small event planning company knows that their business peaks during the summer months. They hire temporary event coordinators and staff to handle the increased number of weddings and corporate events. This allows the core team to focus on high-priority projects.

Use Freelancers or Contractors: Freelancers and independent contractors can be an excellent solution for project-based work or when you need expertise that isn't required year-round. This option allows you to bring in specialized talent for specific projects without having to commit to a full-time hire.

> Example: A growing tech company is launching a new app and requires specialized skills in mobile app development. Instead of hiring full-time employees, the company contracts freelance app developers to work on the project for a fixed term, helping them meet their launch deadline.

Plan for Onboarding and Training: Even for temporary hires, it's important to plan for onboarding and training to ensure that new workers are productive as quickly as possible. Effective onboarding can reduce the learning curve, enabling your seasonal staff to perform at a high level.

> Example: A small food delivery service hires temporary drivers to manage a holiday rush. To ensure that the new hires can hit the ground running, they are given a thorough training session on the app, delivery procedures, and customer service expectations before the busy season begins.

Building a Talent Pipeline

Building a talent pipeline is a proactive strategy for ensuring that you have a pool of qualified candidates ready to fill positions when they become available. By consistently engaging with potential hires, you can streamline your recruitment process and reduce the time it takes to find the right person for the job.

Proactive Recruiting to Have Candidates Ready When Needed

Engage with Candidates Year-Round: Rather than waiting for a position to open, maintain ongoing communication with potential candidates throughout the year. This could include sending regular job updates, offering insights about your company culture, and sharing opportunities to connect on social media.

> Example: A marketing agency regularly posts job openings and company updates on LinkedIn, even when no immediate vacancies exist. As a result, when a position becomes available, they already have a list of qualified candidates who are

> familiar with the company and eager to apply.

Internship Programs: Offering internships is a great way to build a talent pipeline while also giving potential employees a chance to learn about your company. Many businesses have successfully turned interns into full-time employees after the internship period ends.

> Example: A law firm offers summer internships to law students, providing hands-on experience with legal research and client communication. Many interns are eventually hired full-time after they graduate, reducing the firm's recruitment efforts.

Networking and Partnerships: Establishing relationships with local universities, professional organizations, and industry conferences can help you build a talent pipeline. These relationships provide access to top talent before they even enter the job market.

> Example: A small web development company partners with local coding boot camps to offer mentorship and job placement assistance. As a result, the company receives early access to highly skilled graduates who are ready to join the workforce.

Employee Referrals: Encourage current employees to refer qualified candidates for open positions. Employee referrals often result in quicker hires, as referred candidates are more likely to be a good cultural fit for the company.

> Example: A startup tech company implements a referral program that offers bonuses to employees who refer successful hires. This leads to faster and more effective hiring, as the company's existing staff already knows the kind of talent that would thrive within the organization.

Outsourcing vs. In-House Hiring

Deciding whether to grow your internal team or outsource tasks is a major decision that depends on factors such as cost, expertise, and long-term strategic goals. Both options have their pros and cons, and understanding which model suits your business is essential for success.

Deciding Between Growing Your Internal Team or Outsourcing Tasks

Outsourcing: Outsourcing involves hiring third-party companies or individuals to handle certain tasks, rather than bringing those functions in-house. This can be a more cost-effective solution, particularly for non-core activities.

> Example: A small e-commerce company decides to outsource its customer service and IT support functions to a third-party company. This allows the business to focus on product development and marketing, while the outsourced team handles routine inquiries and technical issues.

In-House Hiring: In-house hiring involves recruiting employees to fill full-time roles within your organization. This option allows you to build a team that is fully aligned with your company's mission, values, and long-term goals.

> Example: A marketing agency hires in-house content creators and designers to ensure that the work aligns with their brand. The internal team is more invested in the company's success and culture, making them ideal for tasks that require close collaboration and strategic thinking.

Hybrid Approach: Many businesses choose a hybrid approach, where they keep core functions in-house while outsourcing non-core tasks. This can help balance control and cost-efficiency.

> Example: A small business keeps its core sales and marketing team in-house but outsources tasks such as bookkeeping and payroll to external service providers. This allows them to maintain control over customer-facing roles while benefiting from specialized expertise in non-core areas.

Conclusion

Scaling your team is one of the most significant challenges and opportunities as your business grows. By recognizing when it's time to hire, planning for seasonal and project-based hiring needs, proactively building a talent pipeline, and making informed decisions about outsourcing versus in-house hiring, you can ensure that your business has the right people in place to support long-term growth. Keep in mind that building a successful team is not just about adding bodies to your organization; it's about finding the right people who align with your company's vision and can help take your business to the next level.

Chapter 10: Leveraging Technology in Recruitment

The recruitment process has evolved considerably with the integration of technology, offering businesses innovative ways to streamline hiring, improve candidate experiences, and make more data-driven decisions. This chapter will explore the different tools and strategies that can help you leverage technology to enhance your recruitment processes. We'll cover everything from Applicant Tracking Systems (ATS) to virtual team-building tools, automation, and using data to inform your hiring decisions. In an increasingly digital world, using the right technologies can significantly enhance your recruitment efforts, reduce costs, and attract top talent to your organization.

Using Applicant Tracking Systems (ATS)

An Applicant Tracking System (ATS) is a software application that helps organizations manage their recruitment processes. ATS streamlines job posting, resume screening, and candidate tracking, offering significant efficiency gains compared to manual methods. For small businesses and startups, there are affordable and user-friendly ATS tools that can improve the hiring process and save time.

Affordable ATS Tools to Streamline Hiring

BambooHR: BambooHR is a comprehensive HR management system that offers an intuitive ATS feature. It provides small businesses with tools for creating job postings, tracking applicants, and managing the recruitment pipeline. BambooHR also integrates well with performance management tools, making it a valuable option for businesses looking to combine recruitment and employee management.

> Example: A small consulting firm uses BambooHR to track applicants for various client-facing roles. The ATS helps them review resumes more efficiently, and they can easily schedule interviews through the integrated calendar system. This reduces the administrative burden, allowing the HR team to focus on finding the right candidates.

Workable: Workable is an easy-to-use ATS that caters to small businesses and growing teams. With features like job posting syndication to multiple job boards, one-click resume parsing, and custom workflows, Workable simplifies the recruitment process while allowing businesses to maintain control over their hiring strategies. It also offers integration with video interview platforms, further enhancing the hiring process.

> Example: A tech startup in need of software engineers utilizes Workable's resume parsing feature, which automatically extracts key information from resumes and populates candidate profiles. This automation speeds up the resume screening process, and the

> startup can focus more time on interviewing candidates who best match their job descriptions.

JobScore: JobScore is an ATS designed for small businesses and startups. It's a cost-effective platform that provides job posting, applicant tracking, and interview scheduling features. The tool also offers integration with LinkedIn, Facebook, and other platforms, enabling businesses to reach a broader pool of candidates with minimal effort.

> Example: A marketing agency uses JobScore to post job openings across multiple channels, including social media, and track the performance of each listing. This helps the agency quickly identify which job boards are yielding the best results and refine their recruitment strategies over time.

SmartRecruiters: SmartRecruiters is a robust ATS designed for businesses of all sizes. While it offers more advanced features, it also offers a free tier for small businesses. The platform provides tools for managing candidates, collaborating with hiring managers, and automating communication with applicants, including interview scheduling and status updates.

> Example: A small non-profit organization leverages SmartRecruiters to manage their hiring process for fundraising and event coordinator roles. The system streamlines communication between team members, and the organization can easily assess candidate fit based on predefined qualifications and interview feedback.

Using an ATS reduces the administrative burden associated with hiring and ensures that recruiters and HR teams have access to a centralized system to manage candidates and streamline recruitment. With these affordable options, small businesses can use ATS to their advantage, improving efficiency and enhancing the candidate experience.

Automating the Hiring Process

Automation has revolutionized recruitment by eliminating repetitive tasks and allowing businesses to focus on the most strategic aspects of hiring. From resume screening to interview scheduling and follow-up communications, automation can save significant time and reduce human error, resulting in faster hiring cycles and a better candidate experience.

Leveraging Automation for Resume Screening and Candidate Follow-Ups

Automated Resume Screening: One of the most time-consuming aspects of recruitment is reviewing resumes. Automation tools can help screen resumes based on predefined criteria, such as required skills, experience, and keywords from the job description. These tools can rank candidates automatically and highlight the most qualified applicants.

> Example: A retail company uses an AI-powered resume screening tool that scans resumes for keywords related to customer service, sales experience, and product knowledge. The system automatically

ranks candidates based on how well their resumes align with the job description. This reduces the manual workload and ensures that only the most qualified candidates are moved to the interview stage.

Automated Candidate Outreach and Follow-Ups: After applicants submit their resumes, automation can help you keep candidates informed about their application status. Automated email sequences can notify candidates when their applications are received, when they're shortlisted, or if they're not selected for an interview. These automated responses improve candidate experience by ensuring timely communication without requiring HR personnel to manually follow up.

> Example: A growing fintech company implements automated email responses through its ATS to inform candidates whether they've been selected for an interview or not. This keeps candidates in the loop and ensures they have a clear understanding of their status without

> requiring HR teams to send individual responses.

Automated Interview Scheduling: Scheduling interviews is another process that can be automated using technology. Tools like Calendly or those built into ATS platforms allow candidates to choose interview times based on your availability, eliminating back-and-forth emails to finalize scheduling.

> Example: A small accounting firm uses Calendly integrated with their ATS to automate the interview scheduling process. Candidates can choose from available time slots, and the system automatically sends confirmations and reminders, ensuring that the interview process runs smoothly.

Chatbots for Initial Screening: Some businesses use chatbots to engage candidates as soon as they apply. These chatbots can ask candidates basic pre-screening questions about their qualifications, availability, and salary expectations. The chatbot then records the responses and passes them on to HR for further review, automating part of the initial vetting process.

> Example: A small digital marketing agency uses a chatbot on their career page to ask applicants about their experience with SEO, social media campaigns, and other relevant skills. This initial interaction saves time for HR staff and ensures that only candidates who meet the baseline requirements move forward in the process.

By automating these parts of the hiring process, businesses can reduce time-to-hire, improve accuracy, and enhance the candidate experience, all while saving valuable time for HR teams.

Virtual Team-Building Tools

As remote and hybrid work models continue to grow, team-building has become more important than ever. Technology offers a range of tools that can help organizations engage and build cohesion among remote and hybrid teams. Virtual team-building tools can help maintain a positive company culture, foster communication, and promote collaboration, regardless of physical location.

Engaging Remote and Hybrid Teams through Technology

Virtual Icebreakers and Social Activities: Platforms like Donut (Slack integration) or Icebreaker allow team members to engage in virtual icebreaker activities, helping them get to know each other in a relaxed setting. These platforms facilitate informal conversations and help build connections, especially in a remote work environment.

> Example: A marketing agency with a fully remote team uses Donut to randomly pair employees for informal virtual coffee chats every week. These interactions help employees build relationships across departments, even though they're spread across different time zones.

Collaborative Platforms for Team Projects: Tools like Microsoft Teams, Slack, and Zoom enable seamless communication and collaboration among remote teams. They allow team members to chat, share files, and participate in video meetings, creating a virtual workspace where employees can connect and collaborate in real time.

> Example: A software development company uses Microsoft Teams for project collaboration. Each team has its own channel where they share updates, code snippets, and ask questions. This helps the team stay connected and productive, regardless of location.

Virtual Team Building Games: Online team-building games, like trivia, escape rooms, or Pictionary, can be fun ways to engage remote workers. Platforms like QuizBreaker or Teambuilding.com offer structured team-building activities that promote communication and problem-solving, all while boosting morale.

> Example: A remote customer service team participates in a monthly virtual escape room challenge organized by their HR department. The game encourages team members to work together, communicate effectively, and build stronger

relationships, which in turn improves teamwork and collaboration in the workplace.

Employee Recognition Platforms: Recognition tools such as Bonusly and Kudos allow peers to recognize and appreciate each other's contributions. These platforms make it easy for remote and hybrid teams to celebrate accomplishments, which fosters a sense of appreciation and inclusion, even in a virtual environment.

> Example: A SaaS company uses Bonusly to enable employees to recognize each other for hard work and collaboration. The platform integrates with Slack, making it easy for employees to give shoutouts and rewards to teammates for exceptional performance, no matter where they're working from.

By integrating virtual team-building tools into your workflow, you can create a positive, collaborative culture that transcends the physical barriers of remote or hybrid work.

Data-Driven Hiring Decisions

Data-driven recruitment is the practice of using analytics and performance data to make more informed decisions about hiring and retention. With the right technology, businesses can gather valuable data from their recruitment process, which can improve their hiring decisions, reduce turnover, and identify patterns that lead to successful hires.

How to Use Analytics to Improve Recruitment and Retention

Tracking Candidate Sources: By analyzing where your best candidates come from—whether it's through job boards, social media, referrals, or recruitment agencies—you can optimize your recruitment strategy to focus on the most successful sources. Analytics tools integrated with your ATS can provide insights into where your top talent is sourced.

> Example: A small manufacturing company uses data from their ATS to analyze which job boards and recruiting agencies deliver the best candidates. Based on this data, they prioritize posting job openings on the

boards that yield the highest-quality applicants.

Predictive Analytics for Hiring: Predictive analytics tools can help forecast the success of a candidate based on historical data from previous hires. These tools analyze patterns such as skills, experience, and personality traits of successful employees to identify traits in candidates that may predict future success.

> Example: A fast-growing restaurant chain uses predictive analytics to identify personality traits and work styles that align with their top-performing managers. The system flags candidates who match these characteristics, helping HR make more accurate hiring decisions.

Employee Retention Metrics: By analyzing turnover rates, job satisfaction surveys, and performance data, businesses can uncover patterns that indicate why employees leave. Understanding these patterns helps companies address retention issues before they lead to costly turnover.

> Example: A small law firm analyzes exit interview data and identifies that employees in their junior attorney roles leave after an average of two years. The firm uses this information to adjust their training programs and introduce mentorship opportunities, reducing turnover and improving employee satisfaction.

Candidate Experience Analytics: Collecting feedback from candidates about their experience during the recruitment process helps you identify areas for improvement and ensure that your hiring process is efficient and engaging. Tools like SurveyMonkey can help automate feedback collection from both candidates who were hired and those who weren't.

> Example: A marketing agency uses SurveyMonkey to send candidates a survey after their interview to gather feedback about the recruitment process. The insights they gather allow them to refine their interview questions and improve the candidate experience.

By embracing data-driven recruitment, you can ensure that your hiring decisions are informed, strategic, and aligned with your business goals.

Conclusion

Technology is revolutionizing recruitment, making it easier and more efficient than ever to attract, evaluate, and hire top talent. From using ATS tools for streamlined hiring processes to leveraging automation for candidate follow-ups and data-driven insights to improve your recruitment strategy, the potential benefits are vast. Additionally, virtual team-building tools can foster strong relationships among remote and hybrid teams, ensuring that company culture remains intact, regardless of location. By embracing these technologies, businesses can enhance their recruitment efforts, reduce costs, and make more informed decisions that align with long-term growth.

Conclusion: Building Your Dream Team on a Budget

As a small business owner, one of the most significant challenges you face is building a team that can support your business's growth and success without breaking the bank. The key to achieving this goal lies in adopting strategic, cost-effective hiring practices that allow you to find the right people, onboard them efficiently, and cultivate a productive and motivated team. The strategies discussed in this book are designed to help you streamline your recruitment process and maximize the impact of every dollar spent. In this conclusion, we'll recap the most effective hiring strategies, encourage you to take action now, and highlight the long-term benefits of investing in the right talent.

Recap of Key Takeaways

Throughout this book, we've explored a range of cost-effective hiring strategies that will help small business owners recruit, hire, and retain the best talent without breaking their budgets. Let's summarize the most essential takeaways:

Defining Your Ideal Candidate

Before starting the hiring process, it's essential to have a clear understanding of the type of candidate you're looking for. Creating a detailed job description that outlines the key responsibilities, necessary qualifications, and desired skills helps you attract the right applicants. By clearly defining your ideal candidate upfront, you will avoid wasting time on unqualified individuals and ensure that you're hiring someone who truly aligns with your business needs.

> Takeaway: Spend time crafting a clear, comprehensive job description to attract the best candidates. This foundational

step will help ensure your recruitment efforts are more focused and productive.

Leveraging Affordable Job Boards

When it comes to finding candidates, you don't need to rely on expensive job boards or recruitment agencies. There are numerous affordable or even free job boards that provide access to a large pool of candidates. Platforms like Indeed, LinkedIn, and ZipRecruiter offer options for businesses on a budget to post job openings and screen applicants effectively.

> Takeaway: Utilize free or low-cost job boards to post your positions, ensuring maximum exposure to the right candidates without overspending on expensive recruitment services.

Building a Strong Employer Brand

A strong employer brand can significantly influence the quality of candidates applying for your job openings. Small businesses often have the advantage of creating a more personal and engaging employer brand that showcases company culture, values, and work-life balance. This attracts applicants who are aligned with your company's vision and values, leading to better employee retention in the long run.

> Takeaway: Develop a clear and authentic employer brand to differentiate your company and attract top talent. Showcasing your business's unique culture and values will help you build a loyal team.

Networking and Employee Referrals

Employee referrals and networking are two powerful strategies for finding great talent. Employees who refer candidates tend to bring in individuals who fit better with the company culture, reducing hiring risks and the time spent on the recruitment process. Networking also allows you to tap into a pool of talent through professional associations, industry events, and local community organizations.

> Takeaway: Encourage employee referrals and actively network within your industry and local community to discover top

talent that may not be easily found through traditional job boards.

Screening Resumes Efficiently

Streamlining the resume screening process is crucial to reducing the time and effort required to review applicants. Leveraging Applicant Tracking Systems (ATS) or simply setting clear criteria for what makes a candidate stand out can help automate the process and eliminate unqualified candidates quickly. Automated screening tools allow you to focus on the most promising candidates without spending hours on manual evaluations.

> Takeaway: Use ATS or other resume screening tools to automate and streamline the hiring process. This saves time and ensures that you're only focusing on candidates who meet your specific criteria.

Emphasizing Cultural Fit and Soft Skills

While technical expertise and qualifications are essential, cultural fit and soft skills are equally important when hiring for small businesses. A candidate who fits into your company culture will be more likely to thrive in their role and contribute to a positive work environment. Focus on finding candidates who not only have the necessary technical skills but who also align with your company values and possess strong interpersonal skills.

> Takeaway: Evaluate candidates for cultural fit and soft skills to ensure they align with your company's mission, values, and work environment. This reduces turnover and fosters long-term success.

Leveraging Technology in Recruitment

Utilizing technology to streamline your hiring process is one of the smartest moves you can make as a small business owner. Whether it's using Applicant Tracking Systems (ATS), automating resume screenings, or leveraging video interviewing tools, these technologies can save time and improve the candidate experience. With the right tools, small businesses can compete with larger companies in terms of efficiency and professionalism during the hiring process.

> Takeaway: Use technology, such as ATS and automated interview scheduling tools, to enhance your hiring process and ensure you're operating as efficiently as possible. These tools provide value at a fraction of the cost compared to traditional recruitment agencies.

Providing Competitive Benefits on a Budget

As a small business, offering competitive compensation can be difficult, but there are other ways to provide value to employees. Flexible working hours, remote work options, career development opportunities, and a strong company culture can be just as attractive as monetary benefits. Additionally, offering non-monetary perks like wellness programs or professional development opportunities can help you attract and retain top talent without significantly increasing your expenses.

> Takeaway: Focus on offering non-monetary benefits like flexibility, career growth opportunities, and wellness

programs to make your business an attractive place to work, even on a limited budget.

Onboarding and Retaining Talent

Once you've hired the right candidate, the next step is to retain them. A well-structured onboarding process helps new hires feel welcome, informed, and supported from day one. Providing regular feedback, recognizing accomplishments, and offering growth opportunities within the company will help keep your employees engaged and reduce turnover.

> Takeaway: Implement a solid onboarding program that sets your new hires up for success. Retaining talent is often more cost-effective than constantly recruiting for new positions.

Encouragement to Take Action

Now that you have the tools and strategies needed to build your dream team on a budget, it's time to take action! Start by revisiting your hiring process and incorporating some of the ideas outlined in this book. Whether you're using affordable job boards, enhancing your employer brand, or leveraging technology to streamline hiring, every step you take will move you closer to building a high-performing, motivated team that helps your business thrive.

The most successful small businesses don't necessarily have the biggest budgets; they're the ones that are resourceful and strategic in how they approach hiring. With a bit of creativity, persistence, and the right tools, you can build a team that not only supports your business but propels it toward long-term success. Don't wait for the "perfect moment" to begin—start today and make hiring decisions that will pay off in the years to come.

Take Action Today:

- Start by creating a detailed job description for your next open position.
- Reach out to your employees and ask them to refer qualified candidates.
- Implement an ATS to streamline the resume screening process.
- Begin networking with local professional organizations to identify potential candidates.

Building your dream team isn't just about filling positions; it's about finding people who believe in your vision, align with your company's culture, and bring their best selves to work every day. By hiring smarter, you're setting yourself up for long-term success and sustainability.

Final Words of Motivation

Hiring the right team is one of the most important investments you'll make as a small business owner. The people you hire shape the future of your business, and making the right decisions early on will have a profound impact on your company's success. Yes, the process can be time-consuming and challenging, especially when you're trying to build your dream team on a budget. But remember, every step you take to hire smarter, whether it's refining your job descriptions, implementing technology, or creating a welcoming work culture, is an investment in your business's future.

The path to building a successful team doesn't have to be paved with high costs. In fact, small businesses often have the advantage of being nimble, creative, and adaptable when it comes to attracting top talent. By focusing on efficiency, cultural fit, and leveraging cost-effective recruitment tools, you can build a team that not only supports your goals but accelerates your growth.

Ultimately, the long-term value of investing in the right people cannot be overstated. The team you build today will lay the foundation for the success of your business tomorrow. A motivated, engaged, and talented team can take your small business to new heights, propelling you beyond your competition and helping you create lasting value for both your customers and your employees.

Take the first step today, and watch as your dream team helps transform your business into a thriving success. Your business deserves it—and so do you.

In conclusion, small business owners have the ability to hire smart, build a cohesive team, and set the stage for long-term success without spending a fortune. The right people are the key to your success, and by using strategic and cost-effective hiring practices, you can attract, hire, and retain talent that will take your business to new heights. Don't let the challenges of hiring on a budget stop you—take action, invest in the right tools, and start building your dream team today.

Bonus Resources

Building and maintaining a high-performing team on a budget requires continuous learning, refinement of processes, and effective tools to streamline operations. In this bonus section, we've provided practical resources—templates and checklists, recommended tools and software, and suggestions for further reading and online courses—to help you with your hiring, onboarding, and team management strategies. These resources will provide you with the practical tools and knowledge you need to continue building your dream team.

Templates and Checklists

Creating a standardized process for hiring, onboarding, and managing employees can save you time, reduce errors, and ensure consistency. Below are some helpful templates and checklists that can guide you through each stage of recruitment and employee management.

Job Description Templates

Creating clear, concise, and compelling job descriptions is crucial for attracting the right candidates. A well-written job description provides potential applicants with a clear understanding of the role and its expectations. Here's a basic template for creating effective job descriptions:

Job Title: [Job Title]

- Department: [Department Name]
- Reports To: [Supervisor/Manager]
- Location: [Office/Remote]
- Job Type: [Full-Time/Part-Time/Contract]

Job Summary: A brief overview of the job's purpose and its impact on the business.

Key Responsibilities:
- List the essential job functions and tasks.
- Include specific expectations (e.g., "Manage a team of 5 salespeople," or "Develop and execute marketing campaigns").
- Highlight any required software, tools, or processes that the candidate will use.

Qualifications:
- Required: [e.g., years of experience, specific degrees, certifications, skills]
- Preferred: [e.g., additional skills or experience that would be nice to have]

Compensation and Benefits:
- Salary range: [State the salary or offer a range]
- Benefits: [Health insurance, retirement plans, PTO, etc.]
- Additional perks: [e.g., remote work options, wellness programs]

How to Apply: Include instructions on how applicants should submit their resumes and cover letters, along with any additional materials required (e.g., portfolio, references).

This template can be adapted to any job position in your business. The goal is to make it clear and easy for candidates to understand what you're looking for while also showcasing your company as a great place to work.

Interview Question Templates

Having a set of standard interview questions helps ensure consistency across candidates. Below are a few sample questions tailored to different aspects of the job interview:

General Background Questions:

- Can you walk me through your resume and explain your experience in [specific area]?
- What attracted you to apply for this role?
- Why are you interested in working for our company?

Behavioral Questions:

- Tell me about a time when you had to handle a difficult situation with a coworker. How did you manage it?
- Describe a time when you made a mistake at work. How did you handle it, and what did you learn?
- Give me an example of a project you managed from start to finish. What was the outcome?

Skills-Based Questions:

- What tools or software do you have experience using in your field?
- How do you prioritize your tasks when working under tight deadlines?
- How would you approach solving [specific job-related challenge]?

These questions are designed to help you gauge the candidate's skills, experience, and cultural fit. Remember, you can tailor the questions to the specific role and the qualities you're seeking.

Onboarding Checklist

A streamlined onboarding process helps new employees get up to speed quickly and feel supported as they adjust to your company. Here's an onboarding checklist for you to use:

Pre-Start Tasks:

- Send offer letter and contract for signature
- Prepare workspace (desk, computer, software access)
- Create email accounts and logins for necessary systems
- Set up a company welcome package (swag, handbook, etc.)

Day 1:

- Welcome meeting with HR or manager
- Review company culture, mission, and values
- Provide necessary documentation (tax forms, benefits enrollment)
- Introduce team members and provide a tour (if in-person)

Week 1:
- Set up software and communication tools (email, Slack, project management tools)
- Schedule meetings with key team members for introductions and role clarification
- Assign a mentor or buddy for the first few weeks
- Provide role-specific training and resources

Month 1:
- Review performance and expectations
- Set short-term goals and objectives
- Provide feedback and check-in on progress
- Ensure the employee is integrating into the team

This checklist ensures a comprehensive and smooth onboarding experience that sets new employees up for success.

Recommended Tools and Software

Leveraging technology is crucial for making the hiring and team management process more efficient. Below are some affordable tools and software solutions that will help you streamline your recruitment, team collaboration, and productivity.

Recruitment Tools

Applicant Tracking Systems (ATS)

- **Zoho Recruit**: A highly affordable ATS designed for small businesses, offering features like resume parsing, interview scheduling, and candidate management.
- **Workable**: Known for its user-friendly interface, Workable offers both affordable monthly pricing and robust recruitment tools, including AI-powered candidate sourcing.

Job Board Platforms

- **Indeed**: One of the largest job boards with both free and paid options for posting job openings. It also includes

resume databases for sourcing candidates.
- **LinkedIn Jobs:** A great platform for sourcing candidates and building your employer brand. LinkedIn's tools make it easy to manage job posts and applicants.
- **AngelList**: Ideal for startups and small businesses, AngelList allows you to post jobs and search for talent within the startup community.

Team Management Tools

Project Management

- **Trello**: A simple, visual tool for organizing tasks and projects. It's free for basic use and helps small teams stay on track with deadlines and responsibilities.
- **Asana:** Offers a range of affordable pricing options, and it's perfect for teams that need to manage complex workflows and cross-functional projects.

Time Tracking

- **Harvest:** An easy-to-use time tracking and invoicing tool. Great for small businesses with remote workers or contractors, and it integrates well with project management tools like Asana and Trello.

- **Clockify:** A free time tracking tool that helps small businesses monitor employee hours and project progress. It's particularly useful for contract workers or freelancers.

Productivity and Communication Tools

Communication

- **Slack**: Slack provides an efficient and effective communication platform for teams. Free and paid versions are available, and it integrates with other productivity tools like Trello and Asana.
- **Zoom:** For remote or hybrid teams, Zoom is one of the most popular video conferencing tools. It's available at an affordable rate and integrates well with other platforms.

Document Collaboration

- **Google Workspace**: Google's suite of tools (Docs, Sheets, Slides) allows real-time collaboration for teams. It's free for basic use, and businesses can upgrade for enhanced features.
- **Dropbox:** An affordable cloud storage solution that lets you share and collaborate on documents easily. It's essential for managing large files across remote teams.

Further Reading and Online Courses

To continue developing your knowledge and skills in HR, hiring, and team management, the following resources will help you stay informed and grow as a small business owner.

Books:

- "Who: The A Method for Hiring" by Geoff Smart and Randy Street

This book offers a proven, simple method for hiring the right people for your team. The authors provide practical steps for identifying, interviewing, and hiring top talent.

- "Drive: The Surprising Truth About What Motivates Us" by Daniel H. Pink

Pink's book explores what motivates people at work, shedding light on how small businesses can use intrinsic motivation to retain employees and build a stronger team culture.

- "First Break All the Rules: What the World's Greatest Managers Do Differently" by Marcus Buckingham and Curt Coffman

This book reveals how exceptional managers hire and build great teams. It's especially useful for understanding how to create an environment where employees thrive.

Podcasts:

- HR Leaders Podcast:

Hosted by Chris Rainey, this podcast offers advice and insights into how HR professionals can improve team management and hiring strategies.

- The PeopleHum Podcast:

This podcast dives into HR trends, technology, and best practices with top experts from the field of human resources and talent management.

- WorkLife with Adam Grant:

Hosted by organizational psychologist Adam Grant, this podcast explores how to improve work culture, leadership, and employee satisfaction.

Online Courses:

- EBL Training – Entrepreneurial Training:

This site offers over 400 training programs to help engage your employees and develop management skills.

- Coursera – People Analytics by the University of California, Berkeley:

This course focuses on the power of data and analytics in making better hiring and HR decisions, an essential skill for modern businesses.

- LinkedIn Learning – Recruiting Foundations:

A beginner-friendly course that covers all the basics of recruiting, from writing job descriptions to conducting interviews and selecting the right candidates.

- Udemy – HR Fundamentals:

A highly affordable course that covers everything from hiring and onboarding to employee retention and HR compliance. It's great for small business owners looking to manage their HR processes more effectively.

Final Thoughts

These resources, templates, tools, and learning opportunities provide you with a comprehensive toolkit for building and managing a dream team on a budget. By utilizing these strategies, you can attract top talent, streamline your recruitment process, and maintain a productive and motivated workforce. The right team is one of the most valuable assets to your business, and continuous education and the smart use of resources will help you build a team that drives long-term success.